THE PEOPLE

Reflections of Native Peoples on the Catholic Experience in North America

©1992 National Catholic Educational Association
1077 30th Street, N.W.
Suite 100
Washington, D.C. 20007-3852
ISBN No. 1-55833-117-4

TABLE OF CONTENTS

Art by Gus Antone
Design by Tia Gray

FOREWORD

In this year of our Lord 1992, our Native American sisters and brothers mark centuries of living on this land they called Great Turtle Island, later renamed America.

This publication, written by Native peoples, is intended to offer a reflection on their experience subsequent to the arrival of Columbus and the Catholic Church in 1492. It is offered in 1992 as a call to reconciliation for all inhabitants of "Great Turtle Island" as together we seek to understand the meaning of the Columbus event.

Prayer services and educational lectures can be necessary first steps toward awareness and understanding, but true reconciliation will take place gradually as we get to know each other as brothers and sisters who have one Creator, one mother earth.

As one step in the movement toward reconciliation, we suggest efforts to collaborate on issues such as the environment and the family—issues which are of profound significance to Native peoples and of critical importance to the future of America and the church. In working on corporate projects of such import, we may come to know and appreciate each others' values and gifts, and thus move closer to that true reconciliation and community which are signs of the People of God.

Suzanne Hall, SND
June 1992

CONTRIBUTING
AUTHORS

Marie Therese Archambault, OSF

A member of the Teton Sioux, the Hunkpapa, Sister Marie Therese was born on the Standing Rock Reservation, Fort Yates, North Dakota. She entered the Sisters of St. Francis of Penance and Christian Charity, Marycrest, in Denver, Colorado, in 1957. Subsequently, she earned a BA in Education and an MA in Theology, as well as Baccalaureate and Licentiate degrees in Theology and Sacred Scripture in Rome. Since 1988, her teaching and writing ministries have centered on the area of enculturation regarding Native American religious traditions and the traditions of the Catholic Church, especially in the Archdiocese of Denver and with the Tekakwitha Conference.

Rev. P. Michael Galvan

Presently the director of the Office of Clergy Formation and of the Ministry to Priests Program for the Diocese of Oakland and on the staff of St. Monica Catholic Church in Morgaga, Father Galvan is a member of the Ohlone tribe. He serves as chairman of the board of directors for the Tekakwitha Conference. Father Galvan was ordained in 1977. As well as earning an MA in Christian Ethics, he has a PhD in Christian Spirituality from the Graduate Theological Union in Berkeley. Enculturation in the areas of liturgy and spirituality are the focus of his present work.

Kateri Mitchell, SSA

A sister of St. Anne, Sister Kateri is a member of the Mohawk Nation at St. Regis Reserve, Upper New York. She has an MA in Educational Administration and has had experience in teaching, school administration and pastoral ministry. Sister Kateri has worked for decades developing catechetical training programs for Native leaders, both at the Kisemanito Centre in Grouard, Alberta, Canada, and at the Tekakwitha Conference. She has also served in the Diocese of Fairbanks, Alaska, as director of rural ministry, working with various tribes of Native peoples.

Rev. V. Paul Ojibway, SA

A Franciscan Friar of the Atonement and a member of the Ojibwa People from Minnesota, Father Ojibway presently serves as liaison for and director of the Native American Indian Ministry of the Archdiocese of Los Angeles. Father Ojibway graduated from St. Mary's College of California and completed his

graduate studies at The Catholic University of America and Fordham University. His work encompasses consulting on issues related to urban Native American ministry, media and education, and teaching and lecturing on the contemporary relationships between the Native American, the church and society.

Suzanne E. Hall, SND, editor

Sister Suzanne is not only the editor of this publication, but also its initiator. Currently working with the Office for the Pastoral Care of Migrants and Refugees, Office of Migration and Refugee Services of the United States Catholic Conference, she formerly directed the Department of Special Education at the National Catholic Educational Association. In the latter capacity, she was responsible for the NCEA publications *Integral Education: A Response to the Hispanic Presence* and *A Catholic Response to the Asian Presence.*

CHAPTER I

THE CONTEXT

1992 will cause all of us to pause and reflect on who we are as 20th century persons. The events of the last 500 years manifest a dramatic shift in our understanding of ourselves. In a relatively short space of time, we have moved from viewing ourselves as members of villages, cities or nations to belonging to a world community. Things are simply not the way they used to be. Old patterns and old procedures do not work any longer. Symbols of the past crumble away quickly and, with them, some of our old fears and anxieties die.

Some of these fears and anxieties do not die, however, but continue in new destructive forms. The events of the past few years, as we have changed from a community of European immigrants to a community of peoples from every land in the world, have demonstrated that racism in our country is far from a resolved problem. This quincentennial year challenges us to be mindful, in particular, of the first inhabitants of these lands who remain—the Native American peoples.

The first encounter between Europe and the Americas will be remembered in a variety of ways. A contingent of people will celebrate the "discovery of the New World." Of course, most Native Americans will counter with the questions: "How can you 'discover' a place where people have been living for thousands of years?" and "Was not this 'new' world only 'new' to the Europeans?" Moreover, the arrival of the Europeans brought great destruction and this destruction must be acknowledged if we are to reflect critically on the past 500 years with any degree of honesty.

On the other hand, a group of people will view this encounter as only a negative experience. Their statements will acknowledge only the destruction and devastation which followed this encounter between Europe and the Americas. We cannot deny, however, the great advances in science and technology, as well as the uniting of two great branches of the human race. These are events of an extraordinary order.

For Christians, this encounter brought the Christian faith to these lands. As the bishops of the United States have written in *Heritage and Hope:*

> Convinced of the saving truth of the Gospel and grateful for the sacrifices, care and concern of many missionaries for Native People, we point out "the expansion of Christianity into our hemisphere brought to the peoples of this land the gift of the Christian faith with its power of humanization and salvation, dignity and fraternity, justice and love."[1]

At the same time, we must admit that many of the missionary efforts added to the destruction of the Native peoples and their traditions. We are faced with a complicated situation to which there are no simple answers. The hope of this publication is to provide, from a Native American perspective, a Roman Catholic reflection on the last 500 years. These articles provide a means to help the reader with this process of reflection. The process is one of conversion, since we need to be open to the reality we will encounter. This reality will challenge us to leave behind old answers and solutions, to change our understanding of our common history. When Christopher Columbus happened upon these lands, it was neither a "discovery" nor a pleasant "encounter." Rather, it was a collision of two worlds. The subsequent upheaval brought irreversible changes to everyone involved.

The bishops of the United States in their letter, *1992: A Time for Remembering, Reconciling and Recommitting Ourselves as a People*, give us a clear direction for our reflections:

> We speak as pastors, not only about important issues but first and foremost about a people—about our brothers and sisters whose dignity, culture and faith have too often not been adequately respected and protected by our civil society or our religious institutions. We seek to recognize and respond to the strengths of traditional Indian culture and spirituality, the pastoral and human needs of Native peoples, the many pastoral efforts already underway and the continuing moral challenge of pursuing justice in the face of continuing discrimination.[2]

Our goal is thus threefold: to appreciate the historical reality of what took place in the last 500 years; to seek reconciliation among all peoples in the Americas; and to commit ourselves to work for the dignity and integrity of all cultures.

The writers will argue that a new world was given birth—a world which was unknown both to the Native peoples of the Americas and to the Europeans. For the last 500 years, many have not comprehended or seen this new world. It was not one populated by European immigrants. Instead, this new world is the global community in which we live. It is a community which is still being birthed as the various peoples and cultures of the world interact with and influence one another.

Such recognition demands that we reorient the way we view past historical events. We are challenged to critique and to rise above our particular cultural worldview, whether Native or European, and reflect upon history from a global viewpoint. What took place 500 years ago was beyond the comprehension of all the people involved. In encountering each other, a new world was beginning which involved the peoples of Asia, Australia, Africa, Europe and the Americas.

We need also to be mindful of the nationalities which resulted from the encounter between the Americas and Europe. Such new groups of people call some to designate this encounter "Dia de la Raza" (Day of the Race). The encounter between the Americas and Europe was not one event but has resulted in a new understanding of our world.

The arrival of Europeans in our land resulted, whether intentionally or not, in the vast destruction and oppression of the Native peoples. We must simply think of the tribes lost forever, along with their civilization, languages and cultures. It is possible, then, that in many instances our goal is not reconciliation but an initial encounter of mutual respect and reverence.

It is also critical, however, to recognize that all of us have been wounded by the events of the last 500 years. Reconciliation is possible only if these injustices are recognized and owned. This reconciled community, both Native and immigrant, will proclaim by its very existence the coming of God's Kingdom. In a like manner, there must be the recognition of the good that has resulted from the unity of two branches of humanity and the arrival of the Christian Gospel in these lands. On both sides, there must be the acknowledgment of faults and benefits and the adoption of a global perspective on history. Only then can the conditions for reconciliation engage all of us. Having acknowledged our faults and forgiven one another, we need to commit ourselves to building a world more reflective of the Christian Gospel.

As we reflect upon Native tradition and culture, we will ask ourselves how we can protect the dignity not only of Native peoples but all people. The acceptance of our history must move us to determine that the tragedy of the Americas will not happen again. As we look at who the Native peoples are, at their spirituality, customs and social reality, we will gain the knowledge necessary to create a healthy dialogue between our cultures.

Let us embark then on our journey of conversion, of creating our new global history.

Notes

1. National Conference of Catholic Bishops, *Heritage and Hope: Evangelization in the United States*, Pastoral Letter on the Fifth Centenary of Evangelization in the Americas, Washington, DC, United States Catholic Conference, 1990.

2. National Conference of Catholic Bishops, *1992: A Time for Remembering, Reconciling and Recommitting Ourselves as a People*, Washington, DC, United States Catholic Conference, 1991.

CHAPTER II

WHO ARE THE NATIVE PEOPLE?

As we approach the 500th anniversary of the arrival of Europeans in the Americas, we face some of the same questions which surfaced in 1492: Who are the inhabitants of these lands? How do we understand their cultures, their traditions, their worldviews?

The Arawak, the Native peoples whom Columbus encountered, have long since vanished—victims of the collision of these two worlds. Many Native peoples of the Americas are now a mixture of various cultures. It would not be possible now to appreciate the vast numbers of tribes and diversity of Native cultures in Pre-Columbian times.

Let us begin with how we name these people. In the United States of America, it has been common practice to refer to these original inhabitants as American Indians. In recent years, however, this name has been called into question: Why name a people after a mistaken conclusion? These lands were not the Indies and the inhabitants were not, therefore, Indians. Moreover, the name "American Indians" does not include the northern original inhabitants of the United States, the Eskimos and Aleuts. So, the term does not include all of the indigenous peoples of the Americas.

The term Native American has been used of late. This term usually works but must include Hawaiians, Guamians and Samoans. Is it accurate enough? The best solution would be to call the people by the names they use, i.e., Lakota, Pueblo, Thono O'dom. These proper names designate various tribes, pueblos and nations in the same way as other proper names designate Koreans, Croatians, Egyptians.

The use of tribal names demands an understanding and an appreciation of the diversity and complexity of the Native peoples north of the Rio Grande. Fourteen distinct cultural areas exist in the United States and Canada. These cultural areas break down even further along tribal lines. The United States Bureau of Indian Affairs recognizes some 517 tribes. Among these Native peoples, some 149 languages are still spoken. Since each human language represents a particular worldview, we can begin to see the incredible diversity of Native peoples.

As we come to appreciate the complexity of the question of who these Native peoples are, we are challenged to recognize the ability of these people to survive. It is remarkable that so many tribes, cultures, languages have remained in light of the constant waves of immigrants from Europe, Africa and Asia. It is the vitality of the Native peoples, their religious and spiritual strength, which has enabled them to endure. The Native peoples of these two continents have manifested a remarkable ability to adapt to the many changes following the encounter with Europe. The past 500 years chronicle a history of war, disease, famine, forced removal of tribes and exile, unequal application of the law, broken treaties, oppressive economic and educational systems. As Thomas Berry writes:

> The first basis for cultural survival and renewal for the tribal peoples lies in their awareness of having won a moral victory of unique dimensions during the past five centuries. Many peoples have been besieged in the course of history, many have disappeared from the earth, many have survived over long periods to rise in renewed vigor. It would, however, be difficult to find a people who over such a long period have undergone such destructive influences, yet have survived and preserved their identity so firmly as the American Indian.[1]

How many Native Americans are present today? Let us look at the United States of America. The 1990 Census states that there are nearly 2 million American Indians, Eskimos and Aleuts in the USA. *The Seminole Tribune* states, though, that "there are those who say even that number—three times more than counted in the 1960 census—is not high enough. Census Bureau officials estimate that American Indians in general were undercounted by five percent."[2]

We find, for example, that the Navajo tribe's own census in 1989 counted 169,000 Navajos living on the Navajo reservations in Arizona, New Mexico and Utah. The 1990 census counted only 143,000. In like manner, the Salish-Kootenai Flathead Tribe of Montana noted that tribal records show the reservation is providing services for 10,000 Indians, although the 1990 census counted only 5,130.[3] Thus, we would have to conclude that the number of 2 million American Indians, Eskimos and Aleuts is below the actual number.

The census records state that 685,464 American Indians, Eskimos and Aleuts live on reservation lands. This would leave 1.3 million, or about 65%, living outside of tribal jurisdiction. Many of these live in our urban communities. One of the great challenges is to bring the Native population together in these urban areas, since Native people become the invisible minority in cities. The urban areas with the greatest American Indian populations are Los Angeles, Tucson, New York, Oklahoma City, San Francisco, Phoenix, Seattle-Tacoma and San Diego. A particular challenge surfaces in the cities where many in the Native population are themselves immigrants from their reservations. How do we bring these diverse tribes together?

The people who are landless but native to an area, such as the Ohlone in the San Francisco Bay area, are much smaller in number than the other Native peoples. We need to be mindful of these tribes who lost federal recognition under the government's termination policy. How are these landless Native people attended to?

One common perception of the general population is that all the Native peoples have vast reservations. This is simply not true, especially for those tribes which

6

once lived in what are now our major urban centers. In the light of this misperception, it is important to recall that one of the major sources of identity for most Native people comes from the land. Their relationship to the land, to mother earth, is radically different than the one held by the dominant society. The land is not simply for the use of people, but is to be lived with in harmony and reverence. The land sustains life not only by its resources, but most especially by making people who we are. We can understand, then, the great difficulty when the traditional Navajo people were asked to leave the Four Corners area, where the states of Utah, Colorado, Arizona and New Mexico come together. They faced not only the question of relocation but the question of sustaining their personal identity.

While most of the Native people live west of the Mississippi, sizable numbers are found in North Carolina, Michigan, Minnesota and New York. In fact, the states with the largest numbers of Native peoples are Oklahoma, California, Arizona, New Mexico and North Carolina.

A large percentage of the Native population is young. This large young population, reservation and urban, calls us to examine the strength of the educational system among our Native people. Does it provide Native youth with the skills they will need not only to be successful in the dominant culture, but also to retain their cultural identity and heritage? We must note also that one in four Native Americans is poor. As the United States bishops write:

> Many struggle with the realties of inadequate housing, joblessness, health problems including the disease of alcoholism. While significant numbers of Native Americans have become lawyers, doctors, artists and other professionals, many others live with dashed hopes and bleak futures as a result of discrimination, lack of opportunity and economic powerlessness.[4]

We need to be mindful that most Native people have experienced and continue to experience lack of access to the centers of economic and political power, medical, social service, and religious leadership.

Their initial encounters with Europeans vary among the Native people. For some in the Caribbean and in Mexico, contact dates back 450 to 500 years. Others in the more interior areas or in the far north have had contact only in the last 200 years. This has created a great disparity of experience and subsequent development.

Time is not the only variant which must be considered. Various European groups were engaged in the European colonization of the Americas. Whether Spanish, English or Russians were the colonials also affected the nature of contact. Moreover, European missionaries represented numerous Christian faith communities. Even among Roman Catholics, each missionary group had its uniquely characteristic style. For example, the Spanish Franciscans of the 18th century who evangelized the Native people of California believed that the initial step in conversion to Christianity was the acceptance of the Spanish culture.

Finally, we need to recall that some Native peoples' initial contact was with the American descendants of European immigrants. These Americans saw themselves as natives, not as immigrants. Various ethnic groups also brought the Christian Gospel with them in many disparate ways and look back on these events with various perspectives. It would be difficult to make them all fit together.

Out of the 2 million American Indians, Eskimos and Aleuts, there are more than a quarter of a million Roman Catholics. In the Catholic community there are now two Native bishops, more than two dozen priests, many permanent deacons, 90 sisters and brothers and numerous lay leaders. While these numbers may seem impressive, they have been too long in coming. Moreover, the majority of these religious leaders work in reservation areas. The need for Native leadership in our urban communities becomes even more apparent when we recall that 65% of Native peoples live in urban areas.

One of the major vehicles of the development of this Native leadership has been the National Tekakwitha Conference. The Tekakwitha Conference was founded in 1939 as a means for missionaries to support one another in their ministry among Native peoples. The members of the Conference were primarily non-Native, ordained, religious men who shared with one another the particular joys, challenges and difficulties they experienced in working with Native people. By the late 1970s, the Conference appeared to be going out of existence.

In 1977, the Tekakwitha Conference undertook a major reform and began to admit Native people, lay, religious and ordained, as members. Father Gil Hemaeur, O.F.M.Cap., served as the executive director at the national center in Great Falls, Montana. Over the next several years, the Conference experienced phenomenal growth and became the major voice of Native peoples in the Roman Catholic Church in the United States. Emphasis was placed on developing Native leadership in the areas of religious education, liturgy, lay ministry, urban ministry, and preparation programs for non-Native missionaries. In 1988, at its annual conference, the membership wrote the following Vision Statement which details the lines of development over the ensuing five years.

* * *

Vision Statement

As members of the Tekawitha Conference, we affirm our faith in Christ Jesus and our appreciation for the Native communities in which the Creator has placed us. We make the following statement to call all of God's people to a life of holiness and service sustained by the Holy Spirit and inspired by Blessed Kateri Tekakwitha.

As Native Catholics, we are encouraged by the recognition of our Native cultures, traditions, and languages in the Roman Catholic Church. The beginnings of liturgical inculturation are nourishing our spiritual lives. We are supportive of the work of the Tekakwitha Conference and all ministers who help to develop and support Native ministries. The dedication of our ministers, Native and non-Native, bishops, priests, deacons, women and men religious, and lay ministers strengthens our prayer, our involvement, and our unity. We call for continued support and development of programs for all of our people, especially our youth, that they might be able to appreciate both their Native and Catholic traditions.

At the same time, we recognize that there are certain challenges we face. Addiction to alcohol and drugs is destroying many of our Native people. We need to develop awareness and recovery programs adapted to our Native communities. We need to address the lack of interest in, awareness of, and understanding of our Native cultures by the clergy and by the Church in certain regions of the country. This lack of understanding contributes to a lessening of efforts in inculturation and

Native leadership. Our appreciation of the gifts of women of our Native comunities and their participation on all levels needs to be increased. We need to reach out to those who have fallen away from their Native and Catholic traditions. The youth among us need to feel more welcome and nourished by our traditions. Well-developed family life and youth ministry programs will begin to address the challenge of moral and values education. A stronger Christian community will concern itself with the small numbers of Native vocations to the priesthood, diaconate, and religious life. Inadequate and insufficient adult education hinders our understanding and acceptance of the changes begun by the Second Vatican Council. Moreover, we do not always have a voice in the decision-making processes in our parishes, dioceses, and the Universal Church. Finally, for many of these programs, we lack the necessary financial support.

As a result, we would perceive the following needs in our Native communities: We need to have a greater sense of pride in ourselves, in our clans, and in our tribes. A greater sense of hospitality will help in healing past wounds, in inviting our youth into the Church, and in reaching out to the alienated and inactive. Our concern is for both Native people who live on our Native homelands and in our rural and urban areas of our country. Through increased inculturation and education, we will be able to participate more actively in our faith communities in roles of leadership and service. Our respect for life, the unborn, the handicapped, and our elders needs to be reenforced and supported. Finally, we need to develop our own Native ministries and leadership programs.

To address our needs we must undertake the following changes. We need more Native bishops and leaders. Our youth must be invited to a greater level of participation on all levels of community and church life. Through an increased appreciation of our Native American cultures and gifts, we will be able to help the process of inculturation as Native people become more involved in the life of the Church. With such active participation, there will hopefully be an increase in training programs for lay and ordained ministers and an increase in Native vocations. Since many of our Native communities are experiencing a great shortage of priests, we would like dialogue within the Church to develop creative solutions for ordained ministry. We appreciate the ministry of our Native deacons and call for continued support and encouragement for the permanent diaconate. We need to continue and strengthen our commitment to further the work of social and economic justice, not only for our own communities, but for all people who live on Mother Earth.

We must be strengthened for this task by the many good gifts which we are experiencing in the Church: the active role of the laity, the ongoing dialogue between Native American and Catholic ways, the Tekakwitha Conference, the strong faith life which we share, and the involvement of our young people.

During the next five years, as members of the Tekakwitha Conference, we pledge to address the following problems:

   1. Insufficient religious education programs, Catholic schools, and inadequate numbers of teachers

2. Alcoholism and substance abuse
3. Insufficient youth involvement
4. Lack of unity
5. Low self-esteem

During the next five years, as members of the Tekawitha Conference, we pledge to develop the following five strengths:
1. Our Native spirituality
2. Our unity
3. Our strong family centeredness
4. Our youth involvement
5. Lay, religious and ordained ministries in our communities

* * *

The Conference has continued its growth. In 1989, Mr. Fred Buckles, an Assinibine/Sioux, became the executive director and Father Michael Galvan, an Ohlone, became chairperson of the board of directors. For the first time, the leadership of the Tekakwitha Conference was Native.

> *I like the way our church is now. All we need is for more teenagers to belong. Prayers will help this, through Kateri Tekakwitha who I believe is a saint now.*
>
> **Alberta Francis**
> **Penobscot Tribe**
> **Maine**

The challenges over the next several years will focus even more closely on enculturating the Catholic Christian faith among Native people and the continued development of Native leadership. This question of enculturation is a critical one. We must recall that for most Native peoples, acceptance of Catholic Christianity entailed in various degrees the denial or repression of their Native tradition.

The only way Native peoples can embrace the Gospel is as Native people. In liturgy, catechetics, spirituality, Native traditions must be reflected.[5] Enculturation's theological foundation is the Incarnation. God became human in a certain time and place. In such a manner, the Gospel was manifested. In the same way, the Gospel must be preached to a particular people, the Native peoples of the Americas, in a certain time and place. As Peter Schineller writes, "What inculturation means, in a word, is being fully and truly Christian in a particular, cultural context or situation."[6]

The Tekakwitha Conference is committed to this dialogue. How can we help to enculturate the Roman Catholic faith within the Native peoples of the Americas?

One of the great challenges for the Native community is the preservation as well as the reacquisition of their cultural identity. Many Native people have lost contact with their tribal languages, customs and traditions although, over the last several years, there has been a resurgence in Native tradition. How will we arrive at the authentic tradition? We must be careful not simply to mix together all of various traditions. In order to be faithful to our

traditions, we must rely on our elders. Certain rituals or customs, such as the sacred pipe or the prayer to the four directions (cf. section on Native spirituality), will speak to most Native peoples. These rituals reflect the living tradition of our Native peoples as we enlarge our self-understanding.

As Native people, we are naming ourselves anew as we recall our history, understand our present situation, and move forward into the future. May our journey manifest the journey of all life in our Creator's universe.

Notes

1. Thomas Berry, "The Indian Future," *Cross Currents,* vol. XXVI, no. 2, Summer 1976, p. 135.

2. *The Seminole Tribune,* vol. XIV, no. 2, August 14, 1991.

3. Ibid.

4. National Conference of Catholic Bishops, *1992: A Time for Remembering, Reconciling and Recommitting Ourselves as a People,* Washington, DC, United States Catholic Conference, 1991.

5. Michael Galvan, "Native American Catechesis and the Ministry of the Word," *Faith and Culture: A Multicultural Catechetical Resource,* Washington, DC, United States Catholic Conference, 1987.

6. Peter Schineller, *A Handbook on Inculturation,* Mahwah, NJ, Paulist Press, 1990, p. 122.

CHAPTER III

NATIVE SPIRITUALITY

*T*he Statement of U.S. Catholic Bishops *on American Indians* reads: "The Christian faith should celebrate and strengthen the many diverse cultures which are the product of human hope and aspiration."[1]

In this chapter, then, we will attempt to examine Native spirituality. One of the difficulties which must be considered is the difference between Western and Native spirituality. In most of Western thought, a distinction is made between the sacred and the profane. It is possible to encounter individuals and church communities who distinguish between their secular lives and their spiritual lives. Indeed, even at the level of language, Europeans have different words for "spirituality" and for "religion." Most Native American languages, however, lack such words. Joseph Epes Brown explains this absence of such words as a result of the Native religious experience. He maintains that for Native people "religion is pervasively present and is in complex interrelationships with all aspects of the peoples life-ways."[2]

Another equally important difficulty is the tendency of placing all Native American thought into one category. There is neither one American Indian tradition nor one spiritual legacy. Instead, there is a vast plurality and diversity.[3]

The past several years have seen a great increase in interest in Native spirituality. This is a welcome change after decades of decline in the practice of Native American cultures. There are a number of reasons for this change. Ake Hultkrantz summarizes the phenomenon in the following fashion:

> One is the reawakening of the Indians themselves to new national consciousness, or supernational feelings—called pan-Indianism. They have shown us how a traditional religion can constitute a focus of ethnic identity, and an inter-

tribal Peyote ritual can create a bond of commonness and unity between separate tribes. Another service is the growing realization among educated people that in many respects these religions attain a loftiness and dignity that even surpass that of some of the supposed "higher" religions. The high-god concept and the beautiful symbolism bear witness to this. Finally, the modern concern with ecological problems invite us to a closer observation of the Indians on the religioecological level: the harmonious combination of nature and religion that they have achieved impresses every outsider. They evidence in their way of living and in their religion that human beings have to live with nature, and not against it, as is the case in our modern technocratic societies.[4]

The current resurgence in Native American spirituality also presents us with the difficulty of romanticism. We need to approach Native American spirituality with a critical eye. An understanding of Native spirituality which speaks primarily of the image of the "Noble Savage" does not allow the full impact of these spiritualities to be felt.

Finally, there is the difficulty of the changes in Native American spirituality which have been precipitated by European contact. In the lived experience of many Native people, both Native and Christian spiritualities have been intertwined. Thus, the division between the cultures is unclear. We need to place this alongside the fact for most Native people there is not a division between the sacred and profane but a unity of life.

As we begin, let us center ourselves on the significant relevance of a circle of life experiences. The circle, a sacred symbol for Native Americans, externally and internally bonds a people together into wholeness and oneness. The meaning and strength of the circle is an integral part of a faith journey and life experiences with the sacred, the Creator God who is the center of the universe and all creation. Thus, a richer Native experience leads to a deeper and more meaningful Christian experience. The result of this interconnectedness, interrelatedness and oneness is harmony with God our Maker.

Upon observing the sacred circle, we find that as our faith matures, we continue to strengthen our relationship with the Creator, Christ, self, other people and all creation. We realize that the life of faith is all-encompassing, interrelated and interconnected.

With a greater knowledge of our cultural background gained, for example, through tribal stories and values, traditions and customs, ceremonies and rituals, signs and symbols, we begin to appreciate who we are as gift. When we realize that we have been created in the image and likeness of God, we better understand that all that God has made is good and holy. As the book of Genesis says: "God saw all he had made and indeed it was very good." (Gn. 1:31)

Consequently, the sense of sacredness, respect and reverence for all that God created becomes more meaningful. Our hopes, dreams and visions become enfleshed and we can face our frustrations and brokenness with a healthier attitude. Through prayer and fasting, openness to God's healing action can take place. To restore harmony in our lives, Jesus came to make all things new. With the gift of new life, nourishment, healing and strength in the sacraments, the presence of Jesus among us and the presence of one another in the world today, we as church complete the Body of Christ. Together, we visibly walk the earth to share, to love, to support, to affirm and to heal one another. This is to live in harmony as Native Christian Catholics.

When Native Americans appreciate their identity, new life comes. Many must re-identify with traditional roots through sacred ceremonies and rituals, tribal ways and values. This helps Native Americans better understand Christ in their lives and, subsequently, the meaning of a Native Christian Catholic. Gospel values take on new meaning which calls forth and challenges areas of our Native ways in need of purification, conversion and transformation. Consequently, we experience the strengths of our Native tribal values in an interrelatedness and connectedness with the known Christian values. Rather than the blending of two values, we enjoy harmony, oneness and wholeness in our total life experience. This is expressed very well in the words of Paul to the Ephesians.

> There is but one body and one Spirit, just as there is but one hope given all of you by your call. There is one Lord, one faith, one baptism, one God and Father of all, who is over all, and works through all, and is in all. (Eph. 4:4-6)

Understanding this oneness, we become more aware and more convinced that as individuals we have a responsibility to share the gifts received by continuing Jesus' ministry here on mother earth. We need to do our part to strengthen the Body of Christ. Through a deeper awareness of our interrelatedness and interconnectedness, we can touch the heart of another and another's brokenness. Together we can strive to enjoy peace, love and harmony as the People of God and members of one great family. We can walk this earth with dignity and beauty by sharing in the dying and rising of God as a people of hope.

We must acknowledge, however, the tension between evangelization and colonization among Native people. As is so well-chronicled in *The Church and Racism: Toward a More Fraternal Society*, the church has called for a separation between the civil authority and the spread of the Gospel. The document states:

> The first great wave of European colonization was, in fact, accompanied by a massive destruction of pre-Columbian civilizations and a brutal enslavement of their peoples. If the great navigators of the fifteenth and sixteenth century were free from racial prejudice, the soldiers and traders did not have the same respect for others; they killed in order to take possession of the land, reduced first the "Indians" and then the Blacks to slavery in order to exploit their work.[5]

1992 is going to be a year of reconciliation for all. Native Americans have suffered; however, what has happened, has happened. We need to look forward; we need to forgive our brothers and sisters. All of us—white, black, yellow, red—have one Creator. The Spirit is guiding us all. We have been given a sacred responsibility—to take care of the environment—Mother Earth.

Burton Pretty-on-Top
Native American Spiritual Leader
Crow Nation, Montana

The question becomes focused as to how Native Americans were able to reconcile their acceptance of the Christian Gospel and the reality of contact with Europeans. Furthermore, caution must be exercised so as not to equate the actions and attitudes of each missionary to the collective experience of European contact.

There are examples of courageous individuals who argued for the dignity and integrity of Native civilizations.

The relationship of Native spirituality to the universe is foundational. Among Native peoples, the experience of relationship is critical. We exist in relation to one another, to the other living creatures, to the whole created order. We are called to keep these relationships in harmony. In writing of his experience among the Lakota, Paul Steinmetz writes:

> Lakota Spirituality relates one both to the world of visible creation and to the world of spirits. It forms in us a personal relationship to the Earth so that we treat her with respect and reverence. It is a centering of ourselves in creation through a relationship to the four directions, the foundations of the universe and the place where spirits dwell. Through this spirituality we learn to live in harmony with all creatures. It also puts us at ease with the spirits through accepting their presence and through the offering of spiritual food.[6]

Such an attitude is continually reenacted in the Prayer to the Four Directions. In this prayer, the individual or the group prepares for the sacred by placing themselves in the appropriate relationship with creation.

In Native communities the source of life is breath. Since all words are made of breath, they are living and, therefore, need to be treated with reverence. The words a person speaks are sacred since they convey his or her life. Words carry a power with them. I can still vividly recall how my Grandmother used very few words in her conversation. She stated that an overabundance took away their power. Moreover, she held the written word in some distrust. She felt the words might convey less truth since they were separated from the speaker. As a result, she did not want us to write down our tribal myths. If they were important to us, we would learn them.

In a parallel fashion, the works of a craftperson convey an expression of the Creator's life. Each has a unique quality about it.

Time is not to be regarded as linear, marching relentlessly forward to some predestined goal. Rather, time is cyclical, not in a fatalistic sense but in a positive one. This understanding is reflected in the Native concept of the four ages of a person, the four seasons of the year. As the world goes through the seasons of new life to death, so does the human person. A movement from infancy to old age and death is not tragic; rather, it manifests how the human person is part of the created universe. This recalls the Native Americans' understanding that the circle is sacred. Time is seen as a sacred circle which contains, preserves, sustains and balances. Raymond DeMallie, in his analysis of the "hopelessness" which can be found in *Black Elk Speaks*, explains:

> Lakota culture does not emphasize the irreversible, but rather the opposite: what once was is likely to be again. This was the hope that Black Elk voiced again and again in talking with Neihardt, that together they could "make the tree bloom."[7]

Finally, there is a special and unique quality and intensity in the relationships between living beings and their natural environment.[8] If we were to utilize such an approach, we would begin to discern how Native Americans reconcile colonization and evangelization. The actions of individuals or a group fit into the greater scheme of life. The providence of God, moreover, is not contained in a specific action or collection of actions but, rather, in the entire context. It is the responsibility of the community to focus us continually on placing ourselves at the appropriate time in the appropriate relationships with creation.

We must be careful, however, not to allow for an interpretation of passive acceptance of events, of resignation. Native people have a deep appreciation for the reality of evil, of sin, in our lives. By such means as the Prayer to the Four Directions, we are able to see God's providence conquering evil, sin. Sin does not dominate the universe. God's providence permeates. To live our lives as reflective of the Creator's care, we must lead lives of purification and harmony. If one were to pray with a group of Native people, the depth of the desire to be purified so as to walk in harmony with God would be evident.

I recall the Vision Statement which was passed by the annual Tekakwitha Conference in August of 1988. The statement says: "A greater sense of hospitality will help in healing past wounds, inviting our youth into the Church, and in reaching out to the alienated and inactive."[9]

The providence of God is seen in the life the Creator gives us here on mother earth. The tragedy of the over-identification of European colonization and Christian evangelization does not contradict the care of our Creator. Rather, the triumph of the Gospel can be seen in the faith of Native people and the renewed life of our communities. A certain time period must not dominate the great cycle of life. For in the span of five centuries, we Native peoples have experienced great destruction and are now experiencing great hope of resurrection. Such actions manifest that we are part of creation, as the sun moves from new life to death to new life, as the seasons move from spring to winter to spring. So, our Native and Christian spirituality places its hope in God's providence—that the harmony of life will be maintained.

We pray that as we walk in life from the rising of the sun to its setting and as we journey from sunrise to the sunset for a full life, the words of Micah will echo in our hearts:

> This is what Yahweh asks of you,
> Only this, to act justly,
> to love tenderly
> and to walk humbly with your God. (Micah 6:8)

Some sacred symbols in the Native American world which express and give meaning and relevance in the lives of people will be experienced through prayer.

The sacred circle, brother sun, mother earth, the medicine wheel and sacred drum are for Native people signs of fullness, unity, life and good health.

The gifts of creation are family members and are referred to as brother sun, mother earth, each giving us life.

The sacred objects of the circle, the medicine wheel with its four directions or winds, and the drum with its rhythmic beat in tune with our own heart beat are all sources of strength, wholeness, unity and harmony.

The following suggested prayer services are some ways to enter into some Native American symbolism and a better understanding of Native spirituality.

Prayer 1

Gather in a circle with a lighted candle in the center.

Summer is a time of freshness, of color and of life; a time of growing, of nurturing and of maturing. As we live this summer season, let us share the past events of our lives, enjoy the present moments with friends and with family, and dream the tomorrow. Let us try to live this season to the fullest as we continue to be aware of ongoing personal development. Let us focus on relationships with self, others, the world and creation.

Relationship with self (personal identity). Sit in a circle as each person in turn shares responses to these questions.

What kind of an animal or bird would I like to be? Give one or two reasons why I would like to be that animal or bird.

How do I feel about myself physically, emotionally, socially, spiritually, intellectually?

What can I do to strengthen what I like about myself? How can I develop a greater self-esteem?

Relationship with others. In strengthening our bonds with friends, how open are we to widen our circle to allow others in? What is the "entrance fee" to belonging?

Relationship with the world. Create time with a friend to walk down a street. Observe people. How do I feel when I meet people of other ethnic groups? Do I recognize beauty and integrity in others? What is my reaction or feeling as I greet people and they respond or do not respond?

Share these reactions and feelings with someone.

Relationship with creation. As we observe many signs of life in nature, what is our connectedness with the earth, rivers, mountains, hills, sky, sun, winds?

After these reflections, stand in a circle and join hands as the leader prays: Through our relationships, we can help one another grow more fully and experience life with greater wholeness and holiness.

Prayer 2

As the leader offers burning incense in the four directions and Native American drumming plays softly in background, all pray the following:

O Great Spirit
Whose voice I hear in the winds,
and whose breath gives life to all the world,
hear me! I am small and weak. I need
your strength and wisdom.

Let me walk in beauty, and make my eyes
behold the red and purple sunset.

Make my hand respect the things you have made
and my ears sharp to hear your voice. Make me wise
so that I may understand the things you have
taught my people. Let me learn the lessons you have
hidden in every rock and leaf.
I seek strength not to be greater
than my brothers and sisters, but to fight my greatest enemy—myself.

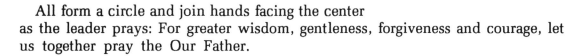

Make me always ready to come to you
with clean hands and straight eyes
So when life fades, as the fading sunset,
my spirit may come to you
without shame.

Prayer 3

In the four directions let us face the center.

N
W   E
S

Four groups are formed, each standing in one of the directions. A lighted candle or burning incense is placed at the center and soft (flute) music is played. Each group in turn prays the direction.

In the East is the rising sun, the dawn of a new day. As we walk the sacred path of life today, help us, Creator God, to grow in wisdom and strength. (short reflection)

To the South, where new and fresh rains come, we ask your help, gracious God, to walk in the ways of goodness and gentleness in heart and speech. (short reflection)

To the West, the place of the setting sun, we thank you, good and generous God, for our day, ask forgiveness for the times we caused disharmony today. (short reflection)

To the North we find courage to walk each day and ask your help to overcome fears and anxieties. (short reflection)

All form a circle and join hands facing the center
as the leader prays: For greater wisdom, gentleness, forgiveness and courage, let us together pray the Our Father.

Prayer 4

As a sign of our baptism and symbol of our ongoing need for healing, we place four bowls of water, one in each direction and play a nature tape of running water. We pray:
Creator, giver of life, bring us to new birth in water and the Great Spirit. Teach us the ways of peace and forgiveness. Help us to respect the differences we see in one another and learn to appreciate them. As we become healers in our

relationships, may we come to wholeness and holiness. Amen.

Each person moves clockwise to each direction/bowl and washes one of the senses as indicated below. Each asks forgiveness (in silence) for the times—by word, action, mannerism or silence—he or she has hurt a person from the different races.

Red Race
Hands
N

White Race **W** **E** Yellow/Brown Race
Eyes   Ears

S
Mouth
Black Race

One or all pray:

Help us, Creator, to walk straight the sacred path of life, hearing your voice and seeing your beauty in creation and creatures alike. Give us the strength and courage, our Creator, to preserve the sacredness of life, of mother earth, and of all creation. Give us the vision to see and admire your beautiful creation. Amen.

Notes

1. *Statement of the U.S. Catholic Bishops on American Indians*, Washington, DC, United States Catholic Conference, 1977, p. 3.

2. Joseph Epes Brown, *The Spiritual Legacy of the American Indian*, New York, Crossroad Publishing Company, 1982.

3. As Joseph Brown states in *The Spiritual Legacy*, "It is evident that in the Americas generally, and in North America specifically, there is neither *an* American Indian tradition nor *a* spiritual legacy, but rather a variety of both."

4. Ake Hultkrantz, *The Study of American Indian Religions*, Christopher Vecsey, ed., New York, Crossroad Publishing Company & Scholars Press, 1983, pp. 95-96.

5. Pontifical Commission "Justia et Pax," *The Church and Racism: Toward a More Fraternal Society*, Washington, DC, USCC, 1988.

6. Paul Steinmetz, *Meditations with Native Americans—Lakota Spirituality*, Santa Fe, NM, Bear and Company, Inc., 1984, p. 12.

7. Raymond J. DeMallie, ed., *The Sixth Grandfather: Black Elk's Teachings Given to John G. Neihardt*, Lincoln, NE, University of Nebraska Press, 1984, p. 56.

8. Brown, op. cit., pp. 2-4.

9. Tekakwitha Conference, *Vision Statement*, 1988.

CHAPTER IV

NATIVE AMERICANS AND EVANGELIZATION

When we, as Native American Catholics, reflect upon the meaning of evangelization for us, a flood of memories and ambivalent feelings is bound to arise.[1] It is difficult to sort out our experiences around this word, evangelization. But, in doing it, we must look at what we can become as Natives and not at what has happened to us as Indians.[2]

It is critically necessary to reflect upon what has happened to us, not only in the Catholic Church, but in Western history. Not to do this would be to deny our very selves and our memory. It would in effect make us hollow people with no identity. If we do not look at both the life and death aspects of our history, we will deprive ourselves of a means for coming to terms with it and of being healed from the psychological wounds it has left within us.

We must admit that our history, in general, has been wiped out of the public memory of the United States of America. We as a people have been trivialized or romanticized out of the conscious memory of most North American people. We must look carefully and long at what this has done to us, especially to our deep inner selves where the image of self is formed and where self-love\self-respect or hatred of self begins. Only after this will we be able to act out of a clear place within us.

The opposite alternative is to react to our history in pain and rage again and again, a normal reaction to such a background as ours. But, in the end, it is not life-giving to repeat this reaction endlessly. Let us choose a dignified way to respond to the memory of our oppression. If we choose otherwise, we risk becoming our own worst enemy, risk allowing the powerful history of our people not to be taken seriously by us and others, and thus to fade totally out of the American memory. We cannot allow this.

The 1992 Commemoration

The commemoration of Columbus' arrival in the Americas calls us to imagine our future in a new way and to take responsibility for what we can become as descendants of the people who dwelt here when he, by chance, landed on a Caribbean island and claimed it for the Spanish monarchs. We owe honor to the memory of our people, those who perished silently throughout the European invasion following 1492 and those who spoke out eloquently, pleading for the survival and honor of our people.[3] We must not let their voices go unheard or unanswered.

Who better than we can hear their pleas and answer them? Our memory of them contains the seed of what we can become, it points to our future. We should celebrate during this year, we should celebrate our survival and build a better future for our descendents. Despite centuries of the European invasion and occupation, attempts to "civilize" us, and the misguided evangelization which accompanied it, we survived, we are still here. This is why the word *evangelization* raises ambivalent and confusing feelings within us. The time has come for us to look at these feelings.

To seek the meaning of the true evangelization of us, Natives of North America, we must take up these tasks. We must:

- Remember, relearn, and integrate our tribal histories and cultures *with compassion* and not seek vengeance upon those who helped to destroy them.
- Listen to the Gospel again with a loving self-respect and dignity.
- Take a fresh look at the tradition of the Roman Catholic Church.

Our history, our identity. Ours is not only a history of oppression. No, it is the history of peoples who lived at least 13,000 years on this continent, by modest estimates, before Columbus arrived.[4] Our people created cultures based upon spiritual beliefs which bound them together in a life of simplicity and balance with each other and with the earth. These cultures were never static; they adapted and changed according to the needs of survival and spirit.

Theirs was not a life of perfection. We do not mean to remember our ancestors as though they were all saints or "noble savages" living in paradise. They were human beings prone to error as all humans yet they, like many indigenous people of the earth, founded and lived a balanced way of life. Many of them became persons of great character and dignity.

Recall the Arawak people who swam out and went in boats to welcome Columbus and his strange entourage as he sailed into their home waters. There is irony in this story of hospitality, for the Arawak unknowingly welcomed their own destruction.

The history of America has been taught in schools and universities as though it were only the history of the European colonies. Many have forgotten our story, but we cannot forget it. If this amnesiac view of North American history is to change, then we must first revive the memories of our people lying hidden within ourselves, for we are the same yet different from our ancestors.

One reason we are different is because we are literate and becoming more and more so. Yet our people, with rare exception, lived in a culture of primary orality.[5] Studies have shown the profound effect literacy has upon people; practically speaking, it reshapes them into different human beings. As literate people, we perceive and learn in ways other than our ancestors did. Given this profound change, we must reappropriate our tribal ways before they die, or before others appropriate them for their own purposes. We know that both of these things have already happened.[6] Studying and reclaiming our religious traditions must be our necessary task if we are to maintain our identity and survive spiritually.

This quincentennial can be the occasion to draw upon the vast energy which lies dormant in this memory of our ancestors rooted within us and in the land of North America. Only we can respond in a way yet unknown on this continent.

The Gospel: an encounter with Jesus. When we read the Gospel, we must read it as *Native people,* for this is who we are. We can no longer try to be what we think the dominant society wants us to be. As Native Catholic people, we must set out with open minds and hearts; then we will encounter Jesus Christ. We must learn to subtract the chauvinism and the cultural superiority with which this Gospel was often presented to our people. We must, as one author says, "de-colonize"[7] this Gospel, which said we must become European in order to be Christian. We have to go beyond the *white gospel* in order to perceive its truth.

When we do this, we shall meet Jesus as our brother and recognize him as one who has been with us all along as the quiet servant, the one who has strengthened us through these centuries. Then we will know that the cry of Jesus Christ from the cross was the cry of our people at Wounded Knee, Sand Creek and other places of the mass death of our people. He was our companion during these years of our invisibility in this society. This same Jesus is the one who challenges us to grow beyond ourselves. This is the challenge of evangelization. If we take up the challenge, we shall sense that he is with us and be glad. This is the heart and core meaning of the Gospel.

The tradition of the Catholic Church. The Catholic Church has an enormously long and varied history of approximately 2000 years. Yet, many of us know nothing of this history beyond what we picked up at mission school or in release-time classes. Frequently, our ancestors were never given a chance to actually choose to be Catholic. Thus, estrangement from the church is common for many of us in our adulthood, we know this all too well. Consequently, as we approach the quincentennial commemorative year, we find we are ignorant of the meaning of the Catholic Church for us, even as we claim to be Catholic.

Furthermore, we have to admit that some of the church's teaching is advanced by humans and, therefore, prone to faults and historical limitations. For example, during the centuries following Columbus's arrival in the Americas, many church leaders did not believe that the "Indians" were human. A Dominican priest named Bartolome De Las Casas taught that the Indians of the Americas were human beings with souls and spiritual capacities.[8] For years, his teaching was banned and considered mistaken.

In recent times the teachings of the great gathering called Vatican Council II (1963-65) were unprecedented for us and for all human beings. In that Council, the Catholic Church opened it doors, its windows, its very self to all cultures and called them to the destiny of Jesus Christ.[9] The Catholic tradition deserves scrutiny by us. Unlike many of our ancestors,[10] we are allowed to freely choose the Catholic faith. Whether our particular tribe chose freely or not, we are called to make that choice anew today. This also is a fresh call to the process of evangelization.

The tasks described above are unsettling ones. If we take up these tasks of looking at our history and traditions, reading the Gospel anew and looking again at the history of the Catholic Church, it will change us. It will call us to be *awake*, not lulled by the comfortable paths of least resistance and safe peace. It will call us to remember and name ourselves in a new way and to reclaim our traditional ways together with the Catholic faith as the real way to spiritual healing and power.

A personal experience. I must clarify my own perspective a little and describe some events which have brought me to this writing. My experience is much like the experience of many Native Catholics. I was born in the Standing Rock Reservation in Fort Yates, North Dakota before Vatican II. My family were nominal Catholics who never practiced the Catholic faith seriously. My brothers, sister and myself attended Catholic mission boarding schools in the Dakotas for our elementary and secondary education because, like so many of our classmates, our parent(s) could not afford to keep us at home.[11] Attending a mission boarding school before Vatican II meant daily Mass and frequent catechism lessons in the Catholic faith.

At an early age I felt called to a contemplative lifestyle and joined the Franciscan sisterhood after high school. I have remained there since. In this life, I have been evangelized in the best ways that the Catholic tradition offers and have acted as evangelizer for others, Native and non-Native.

However, there are two moments of insight which touched me *as an Indian woman* and remain in me as healing memories.

> In the late 1970s, I attended a meeting of the ANCR, the Association of Native Clergy and Religious. A young Native priest dressed casually in jeans, tee-shirt and with long hair pulled back in a pony-tail, also attended. The sight of him brought a new consciousness to me. For the first time it occurred to me that the Catholic Church belonged to us as well. The Catholic Church could take on the look of us, Native people.

Another key event of evangelization centered around the reading of *The*

Sacred Pipe[12] and *Black Elk Speaks*.[13] Through this encounter with Nicholas Black Elk, I was deeply evangelized by a sense of the sacred which came through his life as a holy man and as a Catholic catechist. Especially powerful was his account of the Wanekia vision.[14] For me it was a vision of Jesus Christ as a Lakota man. Something was transformed within me at that moment; it touched me and I wept for my people many times.

I marvel even today that my sense of self as a Native woman was hidden from me. I never even imagined my Native identity and reality as identical with the *Catholic* reality taught me in the mission boarding schools and in convent life. Suddenly, in each instance, upon seeing this young man dressed as my brothers would dress, and upon reading the description of Jesus Christ as an Indian man, these two worlds—Catholic and Native—came together within me. These were moments of evangelization.

It never occurred to me before then that nowhere in my specifically Native world was my Catholic experience embodied. Since that time, I have striven, through prayer and study, to bring these two worlds together within myself even more. Now I am aware that many other Indian people, my classmates and others, share the same experience of separation between these identities.

Evangelization and Enculturation

We can no longer speak of evangelization of Native Americans[15] without simultaneously speaking of enculturation.[16] Our Catholic faith and our Native culture must find a place together. Paul VI has opened and led the way in his teaching *Evangelii Nuntiandi*.[17] For him, evangelization is a call to experience, or to experience anew, the reality of Christ Jesus in the present moment of history, so that the Gospel carries the capacity to be ever new. Evangelization is the witness and proclamation of the presence of Jesus Christ by his followers, based upon their own encounter with him and the inner conviction that only this experience can give. It is only through the evidence of their following the Gospel in such an *outward* way that Christ's way becomes clear, so clear for those who experience this witness of life that they are able to choose or reject the values of the Gospel which he taught.

When the followers of Christ live in a way that reflects his life, they also evangelize all who contact them, no matter where they are. As Paul VI states:

> For the Church, evangelization means bringing the good news into all the strata of humanity, and through its influence transforming humanity from within and making it new....The purpose of evangelization is therefore precisely this interior change, and if it had to be expressed in one sentence the best way of stating it would be to say that the Church evangelizes when she seeks to convert...both the personal and collective consciences of people, the activities in which they engage, and the lives and concrete milieu which are theirs.[18]

It is important to reflect upon the words "transforming humanity from within and making it new." When Paul VI writes the word *within*, he, in the name of the church, calls its "evangelizers" to view the world from *inside* the people it sets out to evangelize. Only at this place inside will the evangelizer know how to call a person within that culture to an interior change. The evangelizers must take seriously the deepest, most dear values, the cultural structures, and ways of those being evangelized. They must see from within the world of the people.

As John Hatcher, a missionary from South Dakota says:

> The Gospel cannot be preached in a vacuum. The people who hear the Gospel have rich cultural and religious traditions which have been handed down for centuries. They have a unique language, value system and way of looking at the world. They have developed customs and laws and distinct ways of interacting. The purpose of the gospel proclamation is not to destroy this heritage. Rather it is to transform it. When a people accepts the gospel proclamation their culture is enhanced. The Gospel gives new vitality to a culture.[19]

Thus, the followers of Christ must seek to enter the reality of those to whom they are sent. When Christ is taught with their inner reality in mind, the Gospel has a chance of making sense to those who hear it. It is Jesus Christ who stands as the center and is the source of every evangelical action or word. The church sets out upon a profound inner journey when it sets out to evangelize.

But evangelization is not only an interior experience of the "consciences of people." When it is genuinely proclaimed and accepted, it will manifest its reality in the "activities, the lives and the social milieu" of the people who interiorize it. Evangelization begins a transformation of the historical reality of the people into a way of life that is compatible with the Gospel and with the best of their own culture. Hatcher, speaking of the exhortation of Paul VI, writes:

> The exhortation instructs missionaries to proclaim the Gospel in a way that does not put pressure on people to receive it. The Gospel is to be presented in a gentle, loving way. Missionaries are to respect the cultural values of the people and respect the pace at which the people can assimilate the message.[20]

It is critical to keep focused on Jesus Christ. By his words and deeds he proclaimed a kingdom of liberating salvation meant to be experienced within a given historical reality. For Natives this is important because even though "he is inseparable from the Church,"[21] sometimes his face is obscured for us by church bureaucracy and its plethora of rules and regulations. This is experienced much like the Bureau of Indian Affairs, as a huge impersonal complex. One can miss the welcoming presence of Jesus within the institutional structures. The vision of the kingdom preached by Jesus and its liberating salvation has in the past often been hidden from Native people due to this particular face and style of the church.

Need to "de-evangelize." In the past the church has obscured the face of Christ through ignorance of or outright dismissal of Native cultures. It has attempted to enter the reality of Native people at superficial levels, almost always from the European viewpoint and perspective. And although archives show that the church missionaries were often far more humane than government representatives when it came to dealing with Native people, what they did was also misguided. Consequently, Native cultures were devalued and rejected by the church's missionaries.

Through this manner of teaching, many Indian people were placed in the profoundly impossible situation of accepting the Gospel for their own good on the one hand while, on the other, having to devalue their culture and thus themselves. It is no wonder that many Native people mistrust all Christian churches and frequently appear outwardly "religionless" in this land. Now, we must undo this attitude and do all we can to reveal the face of Christ, who goes beyond all cultures. This means we must "de-evangelize" Native people.

Bishop Pedro Casaldaliga writes:

> De-evangelizing would mean decolonizing evangelization. The gospel came to Latin America wrapped, borne, and served by a culture at the service of an empire, initially the Iberian Empire. Rather than a pure, supracultural, liberating gospel message, what came was a message that was a cultural import, which for five hundred years has prevented a really indigenous church from developing in Latin America.[22]

Although Casaldaliga speaks from a South American perspective, there is little doubt that, practically speaking, this same process happened in North America. It is clear that no real indigenous church has developed here either. To Native people, the Gospel is often seen as co-opted by the European-rooted, American style.

Yet, this was not the intent of Jesus, as Schillebeeckx attempts to describe in speaking of the early "messianic communities."

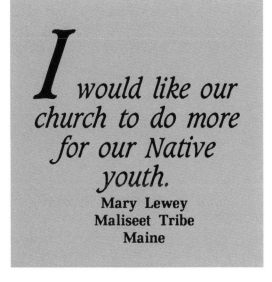

I would like our church to do more for our Native youth.

Mary Lewey
Maliseet Tribe
Maine

> For Jesus the kingdom is to be found where human life becomes "whole," where "salvation" is realized for men and women, where righteousness and love begin to prevail, and enslaving conditions come to an end. Jesus makes the reality of God imaginable in terms of a common participation in a festive and splendid banquet the poor and the social outcasts can share.[23]

In the gospel accounts Jesus finds the ordinary people, even the poor and the outcasts of society, spends time with them, treats them as equals and directs his message to both women and men. This way of acting did not come totally into being once and for all, but whenever it appeared it was something new. Schillebeecbx says:

> The kingdom of God is a new world in which suffering is done away with, a world of completely whole or healed people in a society no longer dominated by master-servant relationships, quite different from that under Roman rule. For this very reason Jesus turns especially to the poor. "Salvation is preached to the poor." To a great degree Jesus' action consisted in establishing social community, opening up communication, above all where "excommunication" and rejection were officially in force: in respect to public sinners, publicans making themselves rich from the poor, lepers and others, whoever and whatever were "unclean." These are the ones he seeks out, the ones with whom he eats.[24]

Jesus, the first evangelizer, through the power of the Holy Spirit and in this moment of history, continues to evangelize and to call Native men and women to experience his kingdom and then to join in proclaiming the reign. This calls for the church's representatives to learn this history for themselves and to teach the Gospel with a renewed understanding of its truth in our context. The Gospel does go beyond the politics of those who preach it. It must be communicated as hospitable and welcoming to all people and their cultures. When this is done, the Gospel casts light upon those cultures and challenges them to a greater destiny, to transcend themselves to become who they really are.

Catholic teaching today. Most recently Popes Paul VI and John Paul II, in their worldwide journeys and in their writing and speeches, have spoken clearly about

the centrality of evangelizing cultures "in depth and to their very roots."[25] The activity of these two contemporary popes and their words is itself evangelizing.

Pope John Paul II addressed Native Americans in Phoenix during his 1987 visit to North America. In that speech and in later ones, he clearly stated the value of Native cultures. He acknowledged the mistakes made in the past by church representatives and called all Native Americans themselves to participate in a new evangelization.

> Your encounter with the Gospel has not only enriched you; it has enriched the church. We are well aware that this has not taken place without its difficulties and, occasionally, its blunders. However you are experiencing this today, the Gospel does not destroy what is best in you. On the contrary, it enriches, as it were, from within the spiritual qualities and gifts that are distinctive of your cultures.[26]

"The Gospel does not destroy what is best in you." When we reflect upon these words, we can begin to realize that we are called to become *precisely* Native within the Catholic Church. We are not to model ourselves after something or someone which we are not, either in religious response, in prayer-style or worship! We must draw deeply from the inner being given us at our creation. It is only by drawing from our own depths where the Great Holy Spirit, the "creative, living source" dwells within us, that we can hope to find our way into the future.

Genuine evangelization. We know that at least one of our ancestors did not identify Jesus Christ as an oppressor. History has revealed that some early missionaries taught in such a way that Nicholas Black Elk accepted Jesus Christ as Savior.[27] The story of Jesus appealed to his imagination for there is much about Jesus which resounds in Native ways: his humility and bravary in facing death, his love and service of the people. This identification can be seen in the great Black Elk's vision of Jesus during his Ghost dance experience:

> Then they led me to the center of the circle where once more I saw the holy tree all full of leaves and blooming....Against the tree there was a man standing with arms held wide in front of him. I looked hard at him, and I could not tell what people he came from. He was not a Wasichu and he was not an Indian. His hair was long and hanging loose, and on the left side of his head he wore an eagle feather. His body was strong and good to see, and it was painted red....He was a very fine looking man. While I was staring hard at him, his body began to change and became very beautiful with all colors of light, and around him there was light. He spoke like singing: "My life is such that all earthly beings and growing things belong to me. Your father, the Great Spirit, has said this. You too must say this."[28]

With this vision of the Wanekia, standing at the center of the Sundance circle, we see Jesus Christ among Native people, as one of us. His presence made the tree at the center bloom. He was surrounded by light. This was the Christ who caught the imagination of Black Elk. It does not matter whether this vision came at the beginning or at the end of Black Elk's life as a catechist. It points to his own encounter with Jesus Christ.

In conclusion, we emphasize the church's recent teaching about respect for cultures. It is unmistakable in the teaching of Paul VI, and even today, his teaching is still fresh and challenging:

> All this could be expressed in the following words: what matters is to evangelize man's culture and cultures (not in a purely decorative way, but in a vital way, in depth and right to their very roots), in the wide and rich sense which these terms have in *Gaudium et Spes*, always taking the person as one's

starting-point and always coming back to the relationships of people among themselves and God....Therefore every effort must be made to ensure a full evangelization of culture, or more correctly of cultures. They have to be regenerated by an encounter with the Gospel. But this encounter will not take place if the Gospel is not proclaimed.[29]

We as Catholic Native people are ourselves called to be the proclaimers of this faith in Jesus Christ, with a true sense of our own Native traditions and within the great Catholic tradition. In the next section we will look at cultural ways of Native peoples which open the way for the Gospel and make its entry smooth.

Ways to the Sacred

What makes it easier for Native people to hear the Gospel? What is it in native cultures that clears the path for the Gospel to be embodied among us? There are many ways and we need to reflect frequently on what they are.

"All my relatives." We are people who always sense ourselves in relationship. Our identity has been passed on from within our family groups and clans. Our people formed cultures marked by deep interrelationship within themselves and outwardly with the earth. Living within community and acting with a primary community mentality comes easy for us. Because of this, we have the potential to easily form circles and communities in which to pray, to play, and to support each other.

When Jesus Christ joins the circle of life, church begins. When we look to Christ among us as our life-giver, our strength and light, and seek to embody this goodness among us, church is formed. When we do this, we enter upon an inner and outer journey which will change our lives.

We must be open to the formation of the life-giving community called into being by Jesus Christ by building upon this strong inner cultural quality of being a relative. Then our natural tendency to be within family groups and clans will be enhanced by the richness of Christ's outlook. We will be strengthened to forgive each other more, to help heal each other, to call each other to service. This is what our culture, in union with the church, as it exists among us, can do to lead us further into the sacred.

Sense of humor. We love to laugh. Through these 500 years we have survived by spotting the humor of human foibles, those of ourselves and those of others. Funny stories abound when our families gather. Furthermore, the traditions of the clowns and jesters is rooted in our community consciousness. Among the Lakota, the Heyoka clown figure is sacred. The one representing Heyoka has been called upon in prayer and visions to do everything backwards so that people will laugh and not take themselves so seriously. This ability to find joy even in hardship and suffering opens us to the gospel life. The sign that the Gospel of Christ is among us will result in a deeper sense of joy.

Generosity. Generosity is a deeply formed quality of our people. It manifested itself in many ways and aspects of our life in the past and does so today in contemporary America. When we visit our city or reservation relatives, or when we go to see an old friend after many years, or when we meet relatives of a friend for the first time, we instinctively want to give them gifts.

Years ago when my mother attended the graduation of my youngest brother from a reservation school, she met there the family of his best friend. That family invited her to their home where they treated her as an honored guest. They gave her simple gifts of all kinds, whatever they considered valuable or thought she might enjoy or need: a tire, some quilting material, a few dollars. She knew instinctively to accept these gifts in a spirit of humility. This is the Lakota way.

The Giveaway is a ceremony which continues to exist, although it stands as totally different from the "white" way. It is diametrically opposed to the views of the smart consumer, so upheld in the dominant wealthy modern-day culture. Yet, the experience of gift-giving comes closest to the meaning of the unconditional love of God for us. This doctrine of the church can best be experienced in a Giveaway ceremony.

Sharing. There is another way of being which is almost second nature to us and this is sharing. Sometimes it even goes to the point of doing without so much in order to share with our relatives who need. When we were growing up in mission schools, we always shared what we had. If one of us happened upon a candy bar, it would be shared with friends, even if each received only one bite! We shared buns and bread which we got in whatever manner. It seemed we were always hungry. We learned from our families that sharing equally was our way of life and practiced it without question. This is not to intimate that our boarding school experience was paradise, far from it. But it is good to remember that even in that strange boarding school environment, we behaved according to the ways we had learned in our homes.

The qualities of generosity and sharing are ways which reveal the generosity of God to us. They help us to see God in each other. One of the most profound moments of evangelization for me was when I received a beautiful blanket at my cousin's Giveaway ceremony. He had been given a great honor in his home state for achievements in Native education. To show gratitude, his family held a Giveaway and Honoring ceremony. When my name was called and a beautiful blanket was given to me, it brought with it a sense of the goodness of this family, my own worthiness and the goodness of life. This experience revealed a sense of the sacred to me.

Such a ceremony could act as a bridge leading one into a deeper understanding of the sacred and of the divine mystery. When we become aware that Jesus Christ is a bridge leading us into a sense of the sacred, a sense that is much greater than we can imagine, then we know the meaning of evangelization.

Other qualities such as hospitality, story-telling, honor, respect and humility have been passed on to us. We must explore these as well and let the memory of these qualities form us today. Those described above are very widespread among Native peoples regardless of tribe and so are emphasized. These qualities— a sense of relationship and humor, generosity and sharing—"make the way straight" for the Gospel to enter and take root among us.

Obstacles to Evangelization

Native codependency. The devastation of drug and alcohol abuse among our people is still evident and stands as a towering obstacle to every aspect of our health. It certainly puts a stop to genuine evangelization. Coping with these forms of abuse saps our strength and puts chaos and negative energy into the interior space needed for the spiritual change and conversion to which evangelization invites us.

There have been courageous moves among Natives all over North America not just to "sober up" but to address the social destruction that generations of drunkeness have wrought among us.[30] Perhaps one of the most pervasive effects of addictive behavior is what we have lately named codependency. This word is variously defined by experts. The following definition is from a professor of counselor education at Ohio University:

> Codependence is preoccupation and extreme dependence (emotionally, socially, and sometimes physically) on a person or object. Eventually, this dependence on another person becomes a pathological condition that effects the codependent in all other relationships....[this] ill health, maladaptive or problematic behaviour that is associated with living with, working with or otherwise being close to a person with alcoholism...affects not only individuals, but families, communities, businesses or other institutions, and even whole societies.[31]

This passage describes well the Native situation in regard to alcoholism and

drug abuse. The addictive substance preoccupies the addicted one, which then causes preoccupation by worried family members. In a sense, we all become preoccupied by the addictive substance whether we are physically addicted or not. Furthermore, the phenomenon of codependency is so widespread in our addictive American society[32] that its detection and remedy among us is hindered because it is condoned in the dominant culture. It is not a generalization to state this: Codependency/ addiction and Native American are not only words, but also co-existent realities in Native memory and awareness which endure even into our contemporary world. We cannot deny that some Native families have escaped this suffering, but not too many.

In the scenario of codependency and addiction, the reality of evangelization is far removed. Yet, the evangelists quickly learn that they step into a pervasive culture of alcoholism in which at least two generations have learned codependent behaviors. Many of these behaviors have become habitual in Native society, so much so that many Native people respond to reality through these learned behaviours. This complicates the situation for a well-meaning Christian minister who comes to serve Native people.

At first, the codependent behavior makes sense to those acting it out because it helps them to survive within an anguished family situation. But what was initially a survival mechanism later becomes socialized into behavior which helps neither the drinking person nor the sober relative. Soon the entire family grows so accustomed to the addictive behavior that an habitual tolerance develops which, in the end, enables the drinking. This attitude of enablement becomes a mind-set which affects the clan, the village and Native society.

Codependent persons try not to cause trouble in an already troubled situation. Codependent persons think: Why challenge the drinking relative when she has stopped drinking for the day? Why bother and upset him when he is at work today? I cannot hurt my father, he has already suffered enough.

They become unable to judge what is tolerance and what is enablement. Soon, they act only to survive. For many Native people desperately seeking to hold a family or clan together in a society that is unfriendly to them, codependent behaviors seem like an easier solution. These behaviors become intertwined with the need to survive. This is particularly true of those who live in urban settings.

Widespread studies have shown that the effects of addiction and codependency in a family are profoundly disfiguring, especially to the self-esteem of individuals. Frequently, this lack of self-esteem takes the form of inaction or inability to act for the good of the family or group. It acts as misdirected frustration, anger and rage, which show up in petty fighting and mistrust of family and group members. There also is a learned, pacifying behavior which transfers over to other situations and takes on the look of tolerance and even long-suffering.

Within church communities, it shows itself as group inability to accept challenges and prophetic voices. These effects spread out to the clan, the village and the Native society. Thus, we cannot exaggerate the reality of codependency in Native life today. In the video *Honor for One, Honor for All*, this societal addiction is graphically portrayed, along with steps for its cure.[33]

Evangelization or any other attempt to bring health is stopped short by codependency because Native people frequently are not acting from a place of health within themselves. They are responding to church workers and activities as people profoundly formed by addictive situations and families formed by codependency. They may appear to be tolerant, forgiving and long-suffering, but one look at the stagnant local church situation says something else.

Natives in this state of mind do not possess the inner strength to take on leadership roles or to allow other Native people to grow in leadership roles. How often have we experienced the "disappearance" of said appointed leader? How often have our groups disintegrated because of conflict? Church representatives can be co-opted into this syndrome. It takes a perceptive and courageous minister, one who has faced his/her own leanings to codependency, to challenge such a situation in a compassionate spirit.

The Gospel sheds light on codependency. Jesus never took the easy way out or ran away from speaking the truth even when it was difficult. In the encounter with the risen power of Christ among us, we can find strength to face this situation and act to change it for the better. As Native men and women, we also must courageously examine our own codependent behaviors, such as excessive timidity due to low self-esteem, fear of leadership, lack of self-confidence, jealousy at another's leadership. We must allow ourselves to see how these behaviors hinder the Gospel from taking root among us. We must ask ourselves if these behaviors keep us from challenging our own church and family members to greater growth.

Paternalism. One area of church life blends quite easily with Native codependency. This is the area of *paternalism*. At first, most Indian people appreciated the kindness of the missionaries. They wanted to help in whatever way possible and frequently did with great personal sacrifice. Any diary or notebook of an early missionary reveals the enormous efforts made to help our people for the sake of the Gospel. But we know now that frequently enough

their idea of *to help* became *to do for.*

Paternalism is frequently an interior structure of codependency deeply internalized by non-Natives and Natives involved in the missionary endeavor. Unfortunately, it describes a relationship which has grown into existence historically between church representatives and the Native people in many places. It also delineates the self-images of both groups and from these images it flows into certain roles played by each. The structure is basically either dominator versus the one dominated or the power-possessor versus client-recipient in need.

Usually, the client-recipient is in need of the "goods" or "power" (material or spiritual) of the possessor in order to survive and therefore must remain in the relationship in order to receive them. This is the relationship of parent and child. One plays the knower and the other plays the ignorant and needy member. The giver easily dominates the receiver.

This becomes *externalized* in the behavior of the Native society. As these behaviors become deeply internalized by both sides and acted out over a long period of time, they slowly become jelled into social structures. The structures endure in time because they result in rewards for both sides. Gradually, this way of relating becomes habitual and comfortable because the relationship fills a perceived need of each. Unfortunately, too often this relationship describes the relationship of the church and Native Catholics.

What began within Native people as a sense of insecurity in a strange religion later led to deepening dependency on the church leaders. The behavior of the leaders did not call forth creative response from our people, instead it made us passive.[34] It did not allow us to perceive ourselves as leaders and dynamic participants in the church.

Hatcher calls paternalism "the greatest obstacle to the development of native leadership." He goes on:

> Paternalism is an insidious disease which militates against the formation of a local Church....It is fair to say that most missionaries today try to avoid the glaring mistakes of the past. However, a new form of paternalism abounds in today's mission field. Missionaries want to protect Indian people from making mistakes and taking risks. They often see themselves as taking care of the Indian people. They want to be sure that the people make the "right" choices when they inculturate the liturgy and develop the "right" spirituality.[35]

Codependent kindness. Although paternalism is a problem in itself, it becomes complex when it blends with the substance codependency of Native people. It becomes even more complex when it is done with great kindness. When this happens, Native people depend even more profoundly upon the church representative and even become addicted to the rewards which their behavior gives. Finally, they believe less and less in their own goodness. At this point, the process of evangelization is totally stopped.

Before evangelization can even be addressed, the church must look into the ways that the Native people of a particular church community have been formed in the paternalistic mind-set and how this, along with codependency, has affected both their ability to really own their own capacities for leadership or allow each other to be leaders within it.

A story by an unknown author illustrates this point:

> A French anthropologist working in Chirapas, Mexico, compared the Indian people (80% of that diocese) to a horse that was feeble, so thin his ribs showed, and was dispirited. People noted that over the passage of time his condition

only worsened. Veterinarians were brought in who prescribed medicines and treatments, but the horse was not healed. Finally, a wise old woman came and looked at the ailing animal. "Untie his hooves," she said, for they were securely bound. So they were untied, and soon the horse was youthful, strong and galloping free.

What may appear as kindness within the paternalistic relationship is really what keeps the "horse's hooves tied," it keeps the people from standing and walking on the strength of their own faith and self-confidence or of allowing others among them to do it.

In the Gospel's light. It bears repeating that a paternalistic relationship has nothing to do with evangelization. Christ approaches all persons as brothers, sisters, as equals. The possessor and the clients are both acting out of a distorted view of themselves. Neither is acting as an adult or as a true follower of Christ. By not calling each other to take equal responsibility in the relationship, the participants remain either as benevolent, incompetent parents or as adult-children. Challenging the other in the spirit of the Gospel and sharing the truth in a mutual way would gradually but surely break this profoundly unhealthy way of relating. Until this break comes, Natives and non-Natives who are involved in this codependent, paternalistic behavior will never experience the reality of an indigenous church.

This style of relating stands in stark contrast to the word of God revealed through the Gospel. This word calls us to a freedom from and far beyond codependency. The church representative should begin gently to root out this form of codependency, first within herself or himself, then look to the community. This is the true call of the church. As Ekstrom and Roberts note:

> The Church seeks to upset the criteria of judgment, prevailing values, points of interest, lines of thought, sources of inspiration and models in life which are in *contrast with the Word of God and the plan of salvation.* With the human person as the starting point and always coming back to the relationships of people among themselves and with God, every effort must be made to ensure the full evangelization of culture, or more correct, of cultures. They have to be regenerated by the encounter with the Gospel. But this encounter will not take place if the Gospel is not proclaimed.[36] (italics mine)

As we Native people begin to sense the strength of our Native heritage within us, the Catholic heritage will find its place and many more will be called to evangelize our own people. This cannot be done until the effects of our addictive society, its widespread codepedency and its interlocking paternalism is acknowledged, first within ourselves and then within Native society. Church leaders also have an obligation to allow the Gospel to enlighten and question their decisions regarding Native communities and paternalism.

Praxis for Evangelization

Praxis is a theological term which means "practice" or "work." It will take work to grow beyond where we are now and to become someone more, i.e., who we are in the church. The following process is a suggested way to begin.

In order for Catholic Native people to experience the fruit of evangelization and take their place as participants in the Catholic Church, the healing of memories must take place. When this begins, the process itself will evangelize, because it begins and ends in the living memory of Jesus Christ among the people.

This process-work is a ministry which must be done in small communities, or circles. Every person in the group must be on an equal basis and have equal time to speak; it is important that each be heard. Native leaders must come forward for training so that they can learn to facilitate this process themselves. Such leadership demands that the person already has begun a spiritual journey of sobriety and has training in the skills needed. The process involves the following components:

Prayer based on Native ceremonies and Catholic ritual.

Revival of the memory of who we were as a people before the coming of Western culture, before the devaluation and the distortion of our self-image. This can be done through appropriate readings, films, prayer, stories, personal memories.

Grieving for what was lost, so that we can move on. Discerning leadership is needed to know when to move on. It involves facilitating the ministry of retelling our stories and revisiting our history, much as was done in the movie "Dances with Wolves." Speakers and listeners are necessary for this healing to begin. This process will take time, and it will result in the gradual healing of negative self-images such as the following:

- Indian self-image: wooden Indian, drunken Indian; cultural shame which is learned and resides on an unconscious level.
- Non-Indian images: a sense of non-forgiveness, feeling badly about being the "ugly American" or the unjust aggressor. There is a need to forgive what was done to our ancestors and to seek healing in the relationship with non-Native people.

Celebrating the new awarenesses that comes with healing.

Naming the way of the future through reflecting: What have we become and what way shall we walk in the future?

As a Native American Christian, I celebrate each day my return from assimilation to spirituality. My identity as a person who breathes, walks and talks with the Creator is my heritage.

Dr. Silver Fox Mette
Jacksonville, Florida

Conclusion

The memory of Jesus Christ as friend, as companion in suffering, as our relative risen and among us, as pilgrim walking and dancing with all of us, will heal us. But not only this. Healing will only take place within the setting of our Native ways and Native memories. From this viewpoint, we will begin to perceive ourselves and Christ in a different way: He will be one of us, he will have a Native face. As these memories intersect, we will experience ourselves, our life, our life-giving stories and ceremonies as forming a new and honorable tradition in the Catholic Church of the future. Only after following such a process will we act from this healed place within and be ready to grow into the future as Native Catholics.

In conclusion, we look to an elder for guidance through the tasks which lie ahead. The simple words of Alfretta Antone as she addressed Pope John Paul II during his 1987 visit to Phoenix express our best motivations:

> We choose not only to survive, but to live fully. We want to live in harmony with all people and all creation. We choose to keep alive for all generations the ways of living carved in the stones and bones of our ancestors. We are open to share and receive whatever is good for the life of the human family with all people of good will....As Catholic Natives, we have come to know Jesus as the Son of God who loves us and lives with us. The Holy Spirit works in many ways through our people.[37]

By allowing the Holy Spirit to move among us, we shall know who we are called to become as Native people and as Native Catholics.

Notes

1. For the quincentennial year many articles and books discussing the result of Columbus' arrival have been printed. For the Catholic viewpoint, see: Leonardo Boff, "1492-1992 Celebration of Penance, Celebration of Resistance," *Creation Spirituality*, Sept.-Oct. 1992, in which he says: "For Native Americans, the Quincentennial is a commemoration of five centuries of suffering and betrayal."

2. *Native* expresses a renewed understanding of ourselves and our history. *Indian* expresses that we were misnamed, along with the shame, the self-devaluation and self-hatred, and ambivalence toward ourselves that was internalized with this name for five centuries. For contemporary Native experience, see: Ted Zuern, *Bread and Freedom*, Chamberlain, SD, St. Joseph Indian School, 1991.

3. W. C. Vanderwerth, compiler, *Indian Oratory Speeches by Noted Indian Chieftains*, New York, Ballantine Books, 1972.

4. Henry Warner Bowden, *The American Indians and Christian Missions: Studies in Cultural Conflict*, Chicago, IL, University of Chicago Press, 1981.

5. See Walter J. Ong, S.J., *Orality and Literacy: The Technologizing of the Word*, London and New York, Methuen, 1982. Stresses the vast change within a human being which comes with literacy.

6. Walter J. Ong, "Selling of the Native Soul," *Christian Century*, 1990.

7. Bishop Pedro Casaldaliga, *In Pursuit of the Kingdom, Writings 1968-1988*, Maryknoll, NY, Orbis Press, 1990, pp. 2-3.

8. Markus Gilbert, O.P., *Bartolome De Las Casas: The Gospel of Liberation*, Citadel Series, Dublin and Athlone, Veritas and St. Paul Publications, 1988.

9. Vatican Council II, *Declaration on the Relationship of the Church to Non-Christian Religions (Notra Aetate)*, 1965.

10. Bowden, op. cit. In Grant's Peace Policy, Indian territories were divided between 13 Christian denominations as part of Grant's policy to civilize Indians as well as to bring the Indian wars to a peaceful end.

11. Canadian Natives have done a considerable amount of reflection on this widespread Native experience of the "residential/board school." See: "Residential Schools: A New Kind of Remembering," *Catholic New Times*, March 31, 1991, pp. 9-13, and the video "Where the Spirit Lives," Anglican Board of Canada.

12. Joseph Epes Brown, *The Sacred Pipe: The Sacred Rituals of the Sioux*,

Bloomington, IN, University of Indiana Press, 1971.

13. John G. Neihardt, *Black Elk Speaks: Being the Life Story of a Holy Man of the Oglala Sioux*, A Bison Book, Lincoln, NE, University of Nebraska Press, 1961.

14. Ibid. A footnote defines Wanekia as "One Who Make Live," p. 137.

15. A recent search of theology library computer files under the title "evangelization" revealed not one of 433 items dealt with evangelization of Native/ American Indian people of North America, although one of Columbus' intentions in 1492 was to claim these "indians" for Christ.

16. See *Effective Inculturation and Ethnic Identity: Inculturation*, working papers on Living Faith and Cultures by Maria De La Cruz Aymes, S.H., Francis J. Buckley, S.J., Charles Nyamiti, William E. Biernatiski, S.J., George A. DeNapoli and Eugenio Maurer, Rome, Pontifical Gregorian University, 1987.

17. Pope Paul VI, *On Evangelization in the Modern World (Evangelii Nuntiandi)*, Washington, DC, United States Catholic Conference, 1976.

18. Ibid.

19. John Edward Hatcher, S.J., *Paul VI's "Evangelization in the Modern World" and the Mission to the Sioux Indians of South Dakota: Theory and Practice*, unpublished thesis, Regis College, Ontario, Canada, 1987, p. 12.

20. Ibid., p. 21.

21. *Evangelii Nuntiandi*, op. cit., p. 20.

22. Bishop Pedro Casaldaliga, op. cit.

23. Edward Schillebeeckz, *The Church with a Human Face*, New York, Crossroad Publishing Company, 1985, p. 20.

24. Ibid., p. 21.

25. *Evangelii Nuntiandi*, op. cit.

26. John Paul II, "Address to Native Americans," *Origins*, NC Documentary Service, October 1987, vol. 17, no. 17, p. 295.

27. Bowden, op. cit.

28. Neihardt, op. cit., p. 249.

29. *Evangelii Nuntiandi*, op. cit.

30. The powerful story of the recovery of the Natives from Alkali Lake in British Columbia, Canada, can be seen in the video *Honor for One, Honor for All*.

31. Patricia Beamish, "Codependency and Individuation," a talk at the American Association for Counseling and Development Annual Convention at Reno, NV, April, 1991. Taken from her handout.

32._____, *The Addictive Society;* Diane Fassel, *The Addictive Organization;* Craig Nakken, *The Addictive Personality: Understanding Compulsion in Our Lives*, A Harper Hazelden Book, 1988.

33. *Honor For One, Honor For All*, op. cit.

34. This passivity is not evident in a Native ceremony where Native people prepare, plan and carry out all aspects of the ceremony.

35. Hatcher, op. cit., p. 93.

36. Ekstrom and Roberto, eds., *Access Guide to Evangelization*, New Rochelle, NY, Don Bosco/Multimedia Press, 1990.

37. Address by Alfretta Antone, *Origins*, Oct. 1987, vol. 17, no. 17, p. 296.

CHAPTER V

A CALL TO NATIVE AMERICANS

Hey-a-a-hey! Hey-a-a-hey! Hey-a-a-hey!
Grandfather, Great Spirit,
Once more behold me on earth and
lean to hear my feeble voice...
Hear me in my sorrow, for I may never call again.
O make my people live![1]

The Native American people is a call to prayer—*O make my people live!"*—a call to return again to the center of our existence, identity and vision. Where is our strength as people except at that center of the circle? There we engage the power of the Creator and know ourselves anew. It is a call to renewal and rebirth. It is a call to create a movement toward fundamental social change within our community. It is a call to change the perception from without,[2] as we move beyond the Columbus event and into the next millennium.

We are a complex, multidimensional community that cannot be characterized in generalizations. We are diverse people with many cultural expressions who live with extremes of poverty, alienation, addiction and death—yet Native Americans excel in every occupation. We live in agonizing loneliness in the city— yet many have the joy of knowing a traditional, family-centered community. Many live in the traditional way while many others have assimilated and adapted to the city's ways. Many of us are interracial or intertribal in parentage. Most of us live in the city, but call a far ancestral place our real home.

This complex of extremes, needs and hopes raises difficult, perhaps impossible, questions: Who speaks for the whole? Who in the Native American community provides for or even receives the response from without to our critical needs and deepest desires? What bridges the extremes?

We are many communities with differing agendas and needs that are sometimes conflicting and contradictory, both within a single community and among several communities. A multitude of cultural, artistic, legal, educational, professional and business organizations reflect the diversity and complexity of Native American success and integration into the dominate society. Yet we do not speak with a unified voice to the dominate cultural, political and civic institutions. For this lack of unity, we pay a high price.

Our call to the Native American communities is to create a new vision. A vision for ourselves, based in solidarity and common purpose for all, including the non-Native American. In an essential way, we are the shadow figures in the "American dream." As such, we have much to say about what it means to be at the edge of the American consciousness. We may never wish to fully enter the mainstream of American life, but we must learn the skills to engage it effectively.

The means for this solidarity can be found in recognizing our own fragmentation, competition and seemingly relentless struggle with one another that can only keep us bound to powerlessness. The call is to return to the most sacred traditions of our grandfathers and grandmothers, and to shape our individual and communal lives in a new way. It is a call to recognize, confront and challenge what divides us.

The first words we say to one another need to be echoed at very turn: "You are my relative!" This is no easy task nor one that will be completed in this generation. It is surely the only one that will lead us toward true liberation and hope in ourselves.

Mending the Circle

This call to the people is toward a renewed hope in the future. The renewal will begin with the acknowledgement of the need for healing, i.e., *mending the circle* of the people. It is call to seek out a vision of unity and advocacy for one another. History can teach much about the depths of our divisions and its impact on the Native American population in North America. Deloria states it thus:

> The Sioux, my own people, have a great tradition of conflict. We were the only nation ever to annihilate the United States Cavalry three times in succession. And when we find no one else to quarrel with, we often fight each other. The Sioux problem is excessive leadership. During the twenty-year period in the last century the Sioux fought over an area from LaCrosse, Wisconsin, to Sheridan, Wyoming, against the Crow, Arapaho, Cheyenne, Mandan, Arikara, Hidatsa, Ponca, Iowa, Pawnee, Otoe, Omaha, Winnebago, Chippewa, Cree, Assiniboine, Sac and Fox, Potawatomi, Ute, and Gros Ventre. This was, of course, in addition to fighting the U.S. Cavalry continually throughout the period.[3]

Solidarity with the traditions of the grandfathers must also be a solidarity with each other in the present, for the sake of the future generations. We need a fundamental mutual support system for justice and freedom to live, grow and express ourselves as we wish. In doing this, we will find economic, social and

cultural integrity within to face the racism, paternalism and systemic oppression perpetuated from outside.

In short, we need to redefine the meaning of "home." A home that guards our traditions and fosters self-determination. We seek the conditions for the empowerment of the people, on the reservation, in the villages or in the city.

"We do not want your civilization," as Crazy Hourse said; we have a duty to rebuild and the right to further our own.

> We did not ask you white men to come here. The Great Spirit gave us this country as a home. You had yours. We did not interfere with you. The Great Spirit gave us plenty of land to live on...you are taking my land from me; you are killing off our game, so it is hard for us to live. Now, you tell us to work for a living, but the Great Spirit did not make us to work, but to live by hunting. You white men can work if you want to. We do not interfere with you, and again you say, why do you not become civilized? We do not want your civilization! We would live as our fathers did, and their fathers before them.[4]

To live as our greatgrandfathers and greatgrandmothers lived anchors our self-determination in recognizing ourselves in a new way and in an ancient way. It may mean changing our minds and hearts, but it must mean the fundamental healing of both *in* our own terms and *by* our own ways. It means confronting the sense of heart and soul that we are a homeless and exiled people, even from ourselves. Again, in Deloria's words:

> Native Americans are the popular American minority group and the white majority deeply believes that Native Americans already have the secret mysteries which will produce a wise and happy life. Therefore Native Americans are plagued with a multitude of well-wishers and spectators hoping to discern from within the Native American communities in which they visit, some indication of their substance of religious experience. This inundation of pilgrims makes it impossible for Native Americans to experience the solitude and abandonment which exile requires in order to teach its lessons.[5]

Chief Seattle once asked, "Who speaks for the land?" It is both a critical question to the non-Native American *and* a challenge to the Native American. Both are called on to speak for the future of our mother, the earth, in this hemisphere, and on this "Turtle Island," North America. For the Native American, the land is more than soil, rock, lake and coast to be "owned." It is alive and enduring beyond our transitory lives.

The land and the people are to be in harmony. It is a dance of uniting the universal and the particular, the light and dark, the past and the future. It is embodied in the ceremony, story and memory of the community and each individual therein. Such a harmony connects our spirituality, social organization, economics and politics into one design that is the will of the Creator and that forms the heart of Native American community.

Thus, the Native American's origin, heritage and power is creation itself. Creation is the mysterious and sacred gift that gives birth and rebirth in the image of the Creator, a sacred life in all its forms. Our gift to be given at this time in the history of this land is a prophet's gift. These are the words of truth that speak for the land and our collective harmony in a way that cannot be ignored or alienated from the national consciousness. The prophetic words we speak will radically conflict with an economics and politics of domination, exploitation and unending consumption of the land. It is hoped as well that these words will radically enliven the vision of the future for all.

To do this, Native American leadership must find a common ground to speak together with renewed purpose and vigor. Our collective task is to engage the dominate culture with strength and determination toward the authentic application of justice, human rights and religious freedom. Ours is the call of fulfilling the moral imperative of self-determination and expression for all.

The Native American also must be awakened to his or her own unique gifts,

dignity and power. This is to live in a "sacred" manner. Historically, both the churches and the government have been afraid of our ceremonies and the power these give back to us. In the past, our ceremony, healers, elders and the holders of our sacred traditions have been killed, legally banned (exiled), or discounted to the emerging generation. They were thought to be behind every Native American political and cultural revival after internment on the reservations in the late 19th century.

The federal government's panic in response to the Native American movement at Wounded Knee is only one example of how the fear of Native American self-determination and cultural renewal is acted out in national policy in our own time. The struggles of the latter part of the 19th century are essentially the same as those in the latter part of this century. When will it end?

Our collective renewal must gain us the power to voice an alternative agenda over against the prevailing dominant political and corporate mind. We have much to say about the ramifications of living and achieving beyond what the earth can endure, but our words conflict with the politics of domestic cultural domination.

As will be shown here, our attempts in the last 20 years to revive our political power and religious freedom brought suffering and intimidation unparalleled in the domestic life of this country since the beginning of the civil rights movement. Such is the fear of losing absolute domination of the Native American and the land. Today, we know that any Native Americans who organize to question seriously and publicly the foundations of federal policy over treaty, land or resources will encounter rejection, anger, and sometimes, violence in pursuit of justice. To this degree, Native Americans are still under the domination of a government that chooses to imprison rather than reason with our individual and communal constitutional rights. Many Native Americans who seek justice will say to the dominate society: Name a treaty, name a conviction of political import or alienation from property rights that has not been compromised out of economic advantage or racial fear. This is substantially our historical experience and contemporary struggle as the original people of this land at the hands of the immigrant. Restorative justice towards the land and thus to our sense of ourselves is critical.

To speak for the land is also to speak for the freedom to be as the Creator made us, Native American or not. When the Native American integration of culture, spirituality and self-identity is understood, then our ceremony and rites of passage will be welcomed and offer an opportunity to recreate ourselves. Then the songs in the darkness will not frighten the non-Native American soul. In short, all our ways that bring us strength and wholeness will enrich the character of American life in ways yet unimagined by both. In the Native American imagination is the power which embraces the symbols, images and experience of life into a holistic, dynamic, engaging spirituality of existence. This is our power as Native Americans and no policy of domination or alienation can disqualify it. Chief Fools Crow spoke of our power:

> We do face the sun and pray to God through the sun, asking for strength to complete the Sun Dance, and that all our prayers will be heard. As [we] continue to do this, we are able to see the sun with our eyes completely open. It doesn't blind us, and in it we see visions. No one should be surprised about this. Wonderful and mysterious things happened at the Sun Dances to prove that Wakan-Tanka's...powers are active in our midst...what makes the real difference is that the pledgers are dancing, praying very hard, concentrating, and calling for God's spirit. People forget that, but what we do brings us great power.[6]

Grief for the Past, Hope for the Future

We live with a grief about ourselves that we seemingly cannot let go of without the fear of losing even more of ourselves in the process. Preliminary 1990 census figures show that over 46% of all Native Americans are age 19 and below. Native Americans, then, have the opportunity and tremendous challenge of creating a meaningful future for our next generation. Unless we do so, the grief will continue. How will we counter the continuing growth in suicide (up over 1000% since 1970), family disintegration and substantial loss of culture by assimilation? Perhaps we fear that we have nothing left to replace the sense of hopelessness and exile so deeply ingrained in the collective psyche and soul of the people. We need a means of passage back to ourselves, to "shatter the illusion of separateness."[7]

How does a community bring an end to grief? How does a community find hope for the future? The Cheyenne holy man Sweet Medicine, in his prophecy about the future of the intercourse between the Native American and early settlers in Native American country, gives a clue. We will need to search for the sacred "stones," perhaps stepping-stones on the path of remembering, healing and hope.

> Those people will wander this way...they will be looking for a certain stone....They will be people who do not get tired, but who will keep pushing forward, going all the time. They will keep coming, coming....They will travel everywhere, looking for this stone which our great-grandfather put on the earth in many places....These will do. You people will change: in the end of your life in those days you will not get up early in the morning, you will not know when day comes....They will tear up the earth, and at last you will do it with them. When you do, you will become crazy, and will forget all that I am teaching you.[8]

Perhaps the first stepping-stone is one of *remembering*. Remembering is full of pain and darkness for, in many cases, it is a memory of overwhelming loss, experienced up to the present. Yet the process of remembering and letting go of the experience of grief's "darkness" is itself the beginning of the healing. Remembering is the task of individual and community alike. Shared memory reconnects all to traditions, values and social organization that foster a "native" mind and heart in the people. It is the task of *waking up* to a deeper sense of self-identity. The prophet's mission always has been one of waking up, rousing, and engaging the community. The prophet calls forth the story of the sacred past and preparation for the future, "to know when our day comes."

The discernment of the future is then a collective event, for it means preparation for the very survival and recreation of the people. The responsibility that our older and emerging leadership takes upon itself is to wrestle with forging a unity of purpose based on reconciliation and cooperation on mutual concerns from all spectrums of the Native American world. Leadership of this kind will bridge the gap between tribal government, urban leadership and national organizations. It may mean that we have a traditional heart and a contemporary mind, because we need to survive, to move the community from a "survival" consciousness, the result of a history of victimization, to confidence in the future. It may mean that we have to create for the emerging generation a new self-identity and show them a commitment to a common purpose. These efforts must not be based on old comparisons, quick accommodations or assimilation if we are to achieve our individual and collective aims.

Perhaps another stone on the path is healing the earth and, in so doing, healing ourselves. This, too, is part of remembering. The act of "remembering" implies not only the past but also a proactive reconnecting, regrounding and recreation of the people. It may mean that we have to re-create our communities, both on the reservations and in the cities, so that they become centered on spiritual renewal, justice and self-reliance. For it is only in such communities that we can unlearn the pathological patterns of self-destruction, codependence and fragmentation. In our renewal we can replace these with the power of our authentic traditions, dignity, respect and a life-affirming ecology of the heart for all living beings. Only Native Americans can provide this experience for themselves and discern the depth of the "restorative justice" due the community as a whole. Only Native Americans know the pervasive effects of the loss of the past, which impacts on the present and delimits the future for them.

The New Vision Quest

Because of the Columbus event, it is the appropriate time to take another look at the history of the continent and the impact of the conquest of the indigenous peoples. It is our *appropriate* time to retell the story from the memories deep within our hearts. From our hearts the words will echo the depth of sorrow and the bewilderment that witness to the crucifixion of our past and present. We cannot take responsibility for the guilt, shame and blindness of a culture other than our own. Nor can we assume that we can heal that which is beyond us. But we must be heard and, as has always been our tradition, welcome yet again the unknown into the center of our lives in hope for the future. What Luther Standing Bear of the Lakota said, almost 50 years ago, is still true today.

> The white man does not understand the Native American for the reason that he does not understand America. He is too far removed from its formative processes. The roots of the tree of life have not yet grasped the rock and soil. The white man is still troubled with primitive fears; he still has in his consciousness the perils of this frontier continent, some of its vastness not yet

having yielded to his questing footsteps and inquiring eyes. He shudders still with the memory of the loss of his forefathers upon its scorching deserts and forbidding mountain-tops. The man from Europe is still a foreigner and an alien. And he still hates the man who questioned his path across the continent.[9]

As a national community, we have been echoing this insight in various ways in the past 25 generations and still we are not heard. The critical question is: Why? The struggle with the answer might help us in understanding ourselves and the dominate culture surrounding us.

Native Americans must confront and engage their future. Perhaps it is even more critical that the non-Native American do the same with even greater urgency. For each, the past must inform the present and assist in the reformation of government policy and moral responsibility toward the Native American and all people of color. Without this reevaluation of the past, the non-Native American majority will not recognize a truth outside its own mythology. The historical illusions about its own origins in this hemisphere will endure and continue to victimize others.

In short, the Native American community has the responsibility to help shape and define a new common ground in the reclamation of our most valued legacy, the land itself. We need to help, exhort, support and encourage non-Native Americans to engage in this mutual rediscovery at the local, regional and national levels, as R. A. Warrior notes:

> The four major issues of American Native politics—religious freedom, land claims, resource management and federal-tribal government relations—are areas in which sincere and educated engagement by non-Native Americans can make a difference.[10]

The Healing Church

Reflection on this Fifth Centenary has provided a unique occasion to stimulate an international exchange on the fate of indigenous peoples in this hemisphere. This discussion includes a call for renewed and effective implementation of human rights, self-determination and protection of all indigenous people. It has also been a call to indigenous peoples to see themselves as interdependent across national boundaries and ideology. Support, encouragement and further challenges must be given to this debate in order for it to impact institutions for more than one year of remembrance.

The Native American community has received renewed commitments at national and international levels. These include the declarations of the Commission on Indigenous Peoples at the United Nations, which has declared 1992 the year for indigenous peoples, and those of the World Council of Churches, aimed at the "decolonialization" of all indigenous people. In the United States, the National Council of Churches, the Roman Catholic Church and many mainline Protestant churches with missions to Native Americans have issued statements of concern.

The Fifth Centenary could be a blessing and the dawn of a new era for Native Americans with action on these commitments. There is great potential for developing collaborative efforts in the transformation of the earth and all its peoples between Native American leaders and the churches. This decision, too, is in the hands of the Native American community to foster and enliven with our unique gifts. R. A. Warrior makes this point:

> There are wounds, across all of Native American country there are wounds.

Wounds that make remembering painful. There are wounds unto death. Wounds are part of our history lessons, the sermons we have heard, songs we are taught, stories we are told. The wounds cry out for healing, for an end to pain. The Church has a role to play in healing the wounds, ending the pain.[11]

The Creator has gifted the Native American with a powerful and gracious spirituality that recognizes and appreciates the sacredness of life. This experience permeates all aspects of Native American life and interaction. The churches, on their part, have had a tremendous impact for good or ill on the functioning of Native American communities since the first baptisms. The contemporary thrust toward inculturation and support for indigenous leadership are positive steps in healing the community. There needs to be an ever-deeper appreciation of our heritage and an education on the impact of the issues on the Native American.

The non-Native American church leadership has taken significant steps in this regard by their recent statements. Since 1977, the National Conference of Catholic Bishops has issued three statements which have attempted to further the development of the national community.[12] The United States bishops have displayed a commitment toward renewal and a sensitivity toward the Native American which needs to be recognized and affirmed as constructive steps in the reconciling of the church with Native Americans and in the reconstitution of the Native American socio-cultural integrity in North American society.

Historically, the effect of sharing our Native American territory among the churches has had devastating effects. Inculturation and the inclusion of traditional rites and symbols are not even possible for many fundamentalist and evangelical Protestant missions at this time in their development. These religious divisions call for dialogue on the role of culture in ecumenical settings, but the authentic and holistic inculturation of the Native American can best be formed in the "mainline" Protestant and Roman Catholic missions and urban ministries which are open to inclusiveness. This is the only means for a broad segment of the Native American community to bridge two worlds in a Christian context.

However, in some cases, Native American Catholic communities are not even allowed ready access to church property to gather. Occasionally, some pastors at the local level still refuse to consider the inclusion of Native American ceremony and traditional language in their own communal worship out of a lack of sensitivity that breeds fear and, unfortunately, in some cases, reflects racism. The resulting anger and frustration of the community is crippling and only reconfirms the marginalization of our most dear and urgent concerns. These experiences warrant immediate concern in the churches and in the wider dialogue between churches in support of Native American Christians' inclusion into the mainstream of church life. Without local support and advocacy, the Native American community in a local church or diocese can again be faced with an even more subtle cultural disintegration at the hands of well-meaning yet biased pastors and church leaders who know only a policy of assimilation and who advocate an uniformity of cultural experience.

Many years ago, Plenty-Coups reflected on how the "Christians" of his day lived out what they taught. His words, though harsh sounding, reflect his anger at the duplicity between word and action which is at fundamental odds with the Native American approach to life. That approach calls for the radical (i.e., rooted) integration of experience into life, spirituality and action, based on communal values. Plenty-Coups observed:

They spoke very loudly when they said their laws were made for everybody;

but we soon learned that although they expected us to keep them, they thought nothing of breaking them themselves. They told us not to drink whisky, yet they made it themselves and traded it to us for furs and robes until both were nearly gone. Their Wise Ones said we might have their religion, but when we tried to understand it, we found that there were too many kinds of religion among white men for us to understand, and that scarcely any two white men agreed which was the right one to learn. This bothered us a good deal until we saw that the white man did not take his religion any more seriously than he did his laws, and that he kept both of them just behind him, like Helpers, to use when they might do him good in his dealing with strangers. These were not our ways. We kept the laws we made and lived our religion.[13]

If the churches are to be believed now, the movement toward inculturation and leadership development must include an ongoing reconciliation with the people. This then becomes a healing of the past and an invitation to Native Americans to mend the circle of their lives *within* the church. The vast majority of Catholic Native Americans and those in other Christian denominations are committed to this inclusion; thus, this is an opportunity for the church. We do not call for a separate life, but only the space and time in which to develop our own ecclesial sense of ourselves that is integrated and grounded both in traditional life and in post-Vatican II theological praxis.

This calls for a reevaluation of missiology and the role of political advocacy for religious and cultural freedom. The substantial lack of knowledge and awareness of Native American spiritual values contributes to the disregard and devaluation so keenly felt in the Native American community. Out of ignorance and, too many times, blatant racism, the dominant culture assumes that the Native American does not contribute to the national trust. This assumption must be confronted by our leadership at every turn and in every expression of devaluation of the Native American experience.

Plenty-Coups reflected on the connection between religious values and political action, on concern for truth and the integrity of the practical application of the Gospel. This challenge confronts our easy compromise and divisions between "secular" life and religion.

The response to this challenge requires a determination on the part of religious leaders to walk with us into an unknown territory and wrestle with issues together. We will need imagination in shaping a new kind Native American ministry both on the reservation and in the city. Quality imagination can create the conditions for a vital, ongoing evangelization and renewal for Christian Native Americans that meet our deepest needs and hope for the future.

Some church leaders consider the effort too much because we as a community are so small. This perception fails to recognize the wider implications for the future of Native Americans and their impact on the nation in shaping the moral and political agenda toward a just society. We are not only the "least of the sisters and brothers of the Lord," but also the Samaritan of today.

We therefore challenge the churches to continue the task of building bridges in education, pastoral ministry and leadership formation. The conjunction between Western Christianity and Native American traditional spirituality, psychology, social organization, ceremony, leadership, medicine, song, dance and art provides the multidimensional groundwork for a richer ecclesial and cultural renewal of the whole. This building process is surely a step to any effective and authentic inculturation process. The Native American community has been in an inculturation process for 25 generations. This is a positive, creative and evocative challenge to American churches to be inculturated themselves as they enter the next century as a multicultural national community.

We call the church to the struggle with us to clarify, in contemporary terms, the connection between Native American traditional spirituality and a theology of justice and liberation in a thoroughly American context. This clarification is essential to the formation of an effective and engaging agenda for action on the issues that impact the Native American as no other segment of the American population. To sentimentalize the former without confronting the latter only recreates the past and impoverishes the future.

The Natural Heart

> The old Lakota was wise. He knew that man's heart, away from nature, becomes hard; he knew that lack of respect for growing, living things soon led to lack of respect for humans too.[14]

What can be the constructive response from the Native American nations to these words of Luther Standing Bear? What can it be from non-Native Americans of good spirit toward the Native American? The answer, perhaps, is that all must struggle with the reality that all of us, though different, have a common destiny. We all have a new, unknown frontier to traverse together in a hemispheric and global context. Such an opportunity is awesome to behold. Native and non-Native will approach the path from different directions and perhaps for differing reasons, yet all must affirm the common path if we are to find a sacred ground together. Luther Standing Bear calls for a new kind of "belonging," a new understanding of "home":

> ...in the Native American the spirit of the land is still vested; it will be until other men are able to divine and meet its rhythm. Men must be born and reborn to belong. Their bodies must be formed of the dust of their forefathers' bones.[15]

The most positive movement is from invisibility to recognition. We all need to recognize and educate ourselves to the historical and contemporary contributions the Native American has made to this country. We, as Native Americans, need to move from dependence, oppression, racism and political disenfrancement to self-reliance and freedom. The development of policies based on restorative justice toward our treaty and land claims, including just compensation for the resources removed from reservation lands, is one significant step. Another step is recognition of our need for the same freedoms that the "other" Americans take so much for granted. We need freedom of access to the means of economic and cultural development.

The New Reservation

Today's Native American is young, mobile and urban—part of a population that has increased by 38% since 1980. Preliminary 1990 census figures project that over 62% of all Native Americans live outside the reservation and the vast majority are clustered in six states.

The reservation, however, is a physical, spiritual and psychological reality that extends into urban life for the Native American. The occupation of Alcatraz Island by Native Americans over 20 years ago raised many questions for the Native American and non-Native community alike, questions not yet answered today. This event, like so many before and since, reflects the government's unequal application of legal and ethical standards among the citizenry. It also suggests an apparent unconsciousness on the part of the dominant society, including the churches, to the enforced marginalization of the Native American.

In their statement on the occupation of the island, the American Indian Movement leaders spoke a truth that few in power wished to recognize, let alone deal with in any constructive manner. The statement echoes the cry of the Native American, from both reservation and city, for a place in the political and social agenda. The leaders found that Alcatraz Island was more than suitable as a reservation, if determined by the standards of federal policy and practice. The island, like the city, is a metaphor of the reservation. All three realities describe the Native American's experience at the hands of the dominant society:

- isolated from modern facilities, and without adequate means of transportation
- no fresh running water
- inadequate sanitation facilities
- no oil or mineral rights
- no industry, high unemployment
- no health facilities
- rocky and unproductive soil, land that does not support game
- no educational facilities
- the population exceeds the land base
- the population, held as prisoners, are kept dependent on others

Futhermore, the leaders of the Movement perceived that it would be fitting for ships from all over the world, upon entering the Golden Gate, the symbolic end of America's frontier, to first see Native American land. This would be a reminder of a truer history of this nation than the current mythology allows. Alcatraz would be a symbol of a continent once the home of "free and noble Native Americans."[17]

The white myth of Manifest Destiny, in all its economic and ideological inflation, is still alive and it affects no other community as destructively as it does the Native American. In its continuance, the present reality is one of unending consumption and exploitation of the land at the expense of Native Americans' basic legal rights and even survival. In their Proclamation, written during the Alcatraz Island occupation, the Indians of all Tribes state:

> Right now, today, we who live on the Pine Ridge Reservation are living in what white society has designated a "National Sacrifice Area." What this means is that we have a lot of uranium deposits here, and white culture (not us) needs this uranium as energy production material. The cheapest, most efficient way for industry to extract and deal with the processing of this uranium is to dump the waste by-products right here at the digging sites. Right here where we live. This waste is radioactive and will make the entire region uninhabitable forever. This is considered by industry, and by the white society that created this industry, to be an "acceptable" price to pay for energy resource development. Along the way they also plan to drain the water table under this part of South Dakota as part of the industrial process, so that region becomes doubly uninhabitable. The same sort of thing is happening down in the land of the Navajo and Hopi, up in the land of the Northern Cheyenne and Crow, and elsewhere....
>
> We are resisting being turned into a National Sacrifice Area. We are resisting being turned into a national sacrifice people. The costs of this industrial process are not acceptable to us. It is genocide to dig uranium here and drain the water table—no more, no less.[18]

How can such a mentality, such a collection of federal and corporate policies as these, be advocated or even defended by any person of compassion? When confronted with the reality of these attitudes, values and subsequent policies, the nation must recognize the Native American alienation from both the land and ourselves. The genocide of the people and the essential culture of the continent is deemed "expendable," long-term, for the sake of profit in the short run.

What the Native American has seen, in many differing ways, is the result of a determined, systemic application of a domestic *Monroe Doctrine* based on racism and the economic exploitation of indigenous people. It is no accident of economics or politics that Native Americans hold in 1991 only 4% of their ancestral lands. It is a determined and successful policy of disenfranchisement Such an approach is itself genocidal to the national soul, just as it is of the Native American's very life and possibility of a future. For the Native American, the earth's ecology is as constitutive of authentic spirituality as are politics and economics. This is the prophetic correction we offer to a nation lost in its pathological consumption of itself. A Lakota chant reflects the reality in radical simplicity: "The earth is weeping, weeping."[19]

The leadership in the Native American community has said in many ways that one cannot truly honor the Native American without knowing the state of the community. This knowledge would include the political, spiritual, social (health, education and welfare) and historical context that presently shapes our self-consciousness and our relationship to the dominant culture. Peter Matthiessen, in the introduction to his book, *In the Spirit of Crazy Horse*, writes:

> The poorest of the poor—by far—are the Native American people. It is true that in our courts today the Native American has legal status as a citizen, but anyone familiar with Native American life, in cities or reservations, can testify that justice for Native Americans is random and arbitrary where it exits at all. For all our talk about suppression of human rights in other countries, and despite a nostalgic sentimentality about the noble Red Man, the prejudice and persecution still continue....We honor his sun dances and thunderbird in the names of automobiles and our motels. Our nostalgia comes easily, since those stirring peoples are safely in the past and the abuse of their proud character, generosity, and fierce honesty...can be blamed upon our roughshod forebears....By a great historical irony, many of these lands [where Native Americans were removed to] were situated on the dry crust of the Grants Mineral Belt, which extends from the Dene people in Saskatchewan to those of their close relations, the Dine, or "Navajo," in New Mexico and Arizona, and contains North America's greatest energy resources. More than half of the continent's uranium and much of its petroleum and coal lie beneath Native American land, and so the Native Americans are in the way again.[20]

Once I Had a Home . . .

Will the city destroy us? Will we become "generic" Native Americans—without tribal-specific uniqueness? Will we become assimilated and, in losing our anger, also lose our past; in losing our land, also lose our identity? In the city, where do we find a home?

The federal government's relocation program has had a devastating effect on the shape and future of the contemporary Native American community. Much of the reality of our present urban life can be traced directly back to the social, cultural and economic disintegration that this assimilationist policy engendered in the people as a whole. We are only now seeing the far-reaching effects of this policy on the cultural and social life of our urban community in particular and the reservation communities in general. The assessment of these effects will shape pastoral ministry for the next generation and perhaps beyond.

The reality for the majority of the urban Native American community is marked by the effects of this policy. It is an experience of invisibility in the midst of many minorities, of which the urban Native American is the smallest. A typical absence of political and social cohesiveness only furthers the sense of isolation and alienation that is both individual and communal. Thus a "new fashion" of racism and prejudice, pervasive in its impact, relegates the Native American still further to the margins where the "victims" of social policy live in poverty, alienation and disintegration without a social contract to sustain them. Matthiessen states:

> After four hundred years of betrayals and excuses, Native Americans recognize the new fashion in racism, which is to pretend that the real Native Americans are all gone. We have no wish to be confronted by these "half-breeds" of today, gone slack after a century of enforced dependence, poverty, bad food, alcohol, and despair, because to the degree that these people can be ignored, the shame of our nation can be ignored as well.[21]

Often, when Native Americans raise their voice in anger, frustration or protest, the response is one of surprise or patronizing bemusement: What do they want now? Why are they so upset—they're taken care of, aren't they? The impact of these attitudes and presumptions serve only to disempower, fractionalize and ignore the fundamental dignity of the Native American.

The fragmentation of Native American organizations, church and cultural groups, and nonprofit programs is also a reality and a source of continued disempowerment. The urban community has been in a survival mode at the extremes for too many years with diminishing funds and representation. It is now a question of survival for one's identity, spirituality, language and traditions. A small ethnic and racial population who, in the main, only know *how* to survive and do not know how *not* to be hungry, isolated and angry. The urban experience is just another exile, just another kind of "trail of tears." The reservation is perpetuated in the city. Both experiences are life-threatening and thus unacceptable. Our collective experience will continue unless there is a fundamental reeducation of the dominant institutions that shape American educational and political life.

The estimates from federal and state government calculate that over 40% of urban Native Americans live in poverty. Many of our best and most effective leaders are committed to caring for the urban poor despite less and less funding. Our people enter an urban darkness without support from the federal government and with urban Native American programs incapable of meeting their needs effectively.

Many of our brightest Native Americans in urban life are assimilated into a non-Native American world and suffer a different kind of isolation and alienation. The Native American world finds this urban reality difficult to accept or deal with. Yet these assimilated Native Americans are perhaps one of our best links to access the centers of power and decision making. The Native American community is thus challenged to struggle with their inclusion in the "real" Native American community. This is no easy task in light of the urgency to preserve, protect and reclaim a tradition so battered by popular sentimentality, distortion and generalization.

Invisibility, fragmentation, poverty, survival and assimilation mark the worst of urban life. On balance, however, are the many Native American leaders on the reservation and in the urban communities dedicated to the social, cultural and economic development of the people. Where there is determined support, commitment and sensitivity to the condition of the community, traditional and contemporary expressions in art, culture, education and socioeconomic advancement abound. These are refreshing reminders of the depth of Native Americans' capacity for adaptation. We are not lacking in strength of character, talent or excellence. What we lack too often is the recognition of models of excellence and the confidence toward self-determination so critical to our advancement.

Creating Who We Are

The future is in the hands of the Native American *for* the Native American. This we must come to believe and respond to with urgency and passion. The children and the elders await the words and actions that show a hope and determination to be free. Neither can wait long. It is not enough for the Native American to proclaim that he or she is right about the origin and fate of this land. Our past proves that if we wait to be recognized for the truth we hold, we die and the land cries out. It is not enough for the truth of our spirituality to be held only by the "traditionalist." Nor is it enough to protect the remanent of the treasure of Native American life from further disintegration.

If we do not embrace the future with the power of our many cultures, the lamentation for the past will consume us. It is not enough to remember the past as we would like it, or to create a sacred treasure house of indigenous "traditions" to grow rigid. If we also do not live, teach and renew our tradition, it will be taken from us or, worse, diluted into a pale imitations of the truth.

So we return to the question: How much is enough? It is just and morally imperative *now* for the political, social and religious institutions in America to ensure that Native Americans have the opportunity to live as they wish. These institutions must assure that we have the conditions for restorative justice for the sacrifice of this hemisphere. It is enough that all Native Americans have the opportunity to live with dignity on the land. It is enough that every Native American have access to health, education, social and cultural advancement. This must be on our own terms because we have a right to be who we are made to be by the Creator.

Federal policy and the dominant cultural institutions are guided by the notion that it is only by "civilizing," "enculturating" or "assimilating" will the Native American fit within the confines of American society. We suggest that an athentic history of this land will be written only when the dominate culture recognizes that without justice to the Native American, this society is lost in its own contrived truth about itself. Even more importantly, this authentic history, taught as our common heritage, will shape a new consciousness about ourselves.

Finally, perhaps, we will address as a national society the need of a people to dominate that which is different, prior or challenging to the central myth. Only then, perhaps, the Native American will find the freedom from outside dominance to begin a healing process. The Native American, in turn, can and most certainly will impact the healing of our nation obsessed with the illusions of absolute power over the land and its original people. Both Native American and the sojourners on this continent will then be able to find a sacred home together in harmony and rhythm with the heart of our Creator.

Aho, Aho, let it be so!

Notes

1. John G. Neihardt, *Black Elk Speaks,* New York, Morrow, 1932, pp. 232-34.

2. Robert Allen Warrior, "Indian Issues and Romantic Solidarity," *Christianity and Crisis,* February 4, 1991.

3. Vine Deloria, Jr., *Custer Died for Your Sins: An Indian Manifesto,* New York, MacMillan, 1969, p. 29.

4. Crazy Horse (Lakota), cited in T.C. McLuhan, ed., *Touch the Earth,* New York, Promontory Press, 1971.

5. Vine Deloria, Jr., "Out of Chaos," *Parabola Magazine,* 1989, p. 22.

6. Chief Frank Fools Crow, *Fools Crow,* T.E. Mails, ed., Garden City, NY, Doubleday, 1979, p. 199.

7. Black Elk, *The Sacred Pipe,* J.E. Brown, ed., New York, Penquin Press, 1953.

8. Sweet Medicine (Cheyenne), cited in T.C. McLuhan, ed., *Touch the Earth,* ibid.

9. Luther Standing Bear (Lakota), *Land of the Spotted Eagle,* Lincoln, NE, University of Nebraska Press, 1933.

10. R.A. Warrior, op. cit., p. 8.

11. R.A. Warrior, "Canaanites, Cowboys, and Indians," *Christianity in Crisis,* September 1989, p. 261 ff.

12. National Conference of Catholic Bishops (NCCB), *Statement of the U.S. Catholic Bishops on American Indians,* 1977; *Heritage and Hope: Evangelization in the United States: Pastoral Letter on the Fifth Centenary of Evangelization in the Americas,* November 1990; and 1992: *A Time for Remembering, Reconciling and Recommitting Ourselves as a People: Pastoral Reflections on the Fifth Centenary and Native American People,* November 1991, Washington, DC, United States Catholic Conference.

13. Plenty-Coups (Crow), cited in T.C.McLuhan, op. cit.

14. Luther Standing Bear, op. cit.

15. Ibid.

16. "Progress Report on the Feasibility Study for a National Indian Policy Development," Washington, DC, George Washington University, August 1991.

17. *Proclmation: To the Great White Father and All His People,* written by "Indians of All Tribes," Alcatraz Island Occupation, cited in T.C. McLuhan, op. cit., p. 164.

18. P. Matthiessen, *In the Spirit of Crazy Horse,* New York, Viking Press, 1991.

19. Traditional Lakota chant, cited in T.C. McLuhan, op. cit.

20. P. Matthiessen, op. cit., p. xxii.
21. Ibid., p. xii.

CHAPTER VI

A CALL TO THE CHURCH

Let our Sisters and Brothers hear us!

They...brought us parrots and balls of cotton and spears and many other things, which they exchanged for the glass beads and hawk's bells. They willingly traded everything they owned....They were well-built, with good bodies and handsome features....They do not bear arms, and do not know them, for I showed them a sword, they took it by the edge and cut themselves out of ignorance. They have no iron. Their spears are made of cane....They would make fine servants....With fifty men we could subjugate them all and make them do whatever we want.[1]

This passage from Christopher Columbus' journal notes the beginning of our encounter with the European and his church. We ask now, after 25 generations of this encounter: What has changed? What will change?

We call for change. The call to the church today by the Native American is an urgent one. It is also an invitation—to see, hear and walk with us in the search for a common path into the next millennium. For the last 25 generations we have called to the church to hear as we hear and to see what we see as the indigenous peoples of this hemisphere.

The Fifth Centenary is an excellent and unrepeatable occasion to reflect critically as a church on the roots of our historical identity. It is a time to deliberate on our future as peoples with a common faith that informs our connection to each other and to this land. We need to turn this so-called "celebration" of Columbus into a time for meditation. We see this as an ethical obligation. The conquest of our Turtle Island, begun by Columbus and completed by those who followed, is one of the most significant events in the history of humankind. Can we remain indifferent at this time in our collective history?

Luis N. Rivera-Pagan, in his excellent reflection on the Columbus event, states:

[The discovery of America] is certainly the genesis of modern Christendom as a world phenomenon. In 1492, history underwent a decisive overturn with significant implications for the future of humankind. During the first seventy-five years after the discovery of America, Europe acquired knowledge of more lands than in the preceding millennium and laid the foundations for its world hegemony.[2]

Because of its historical role as a participant in the domination of this hemisphere, the church has now a foundational role to play in creating the conditions for a renewed Native American community. We call for a partnership in the struggle against the injustices of economic, social and religious oppression that have significant implications for all peoples of color. If the church is to be involved in the struggles of the Native American of today, the partnership needs to be based on solidarity. We call on the church to foster a unified urban ministry.

Solidarity in ministry. The renewal of ministry with the Native American must be based on a unity of perception in addressing our most urgent needs, typified by the lowest level of income, education, health care and life expectancy, and the highest levels of drug and alcohol addiction and suicide of any racial or ethnic group of citizens in North America.

An urban ministry. Over 50% of all Native Americans are urban and invisible. We experience ourselves as the soul of the land with no face or name in our parishes, programs or institutions. Furthermore, both on the reservation and in the city we are too often passive participants in the creation of our faith communities. We need to actively participate in the church's vital urban ministry

Urban Ministry: A New Cycle of Life?

The American Catholic Church is now, more than ever before, a multi-ethnic fabric of racial and cultural minorities. This reality will change the shape and direction of the church well into the next century. The minority experience begs for new approaches and methods of evangelization. The development of a culturally centered evangelization process will impact the ministerial, educational, liturgical and pastoral adaptation experienced by the Native American community. In this, the Native Catholic community, with our African American, Hispanic, Asian and Euro-American sisters and brothers, can creatively help the American church in its evolution into the next millennium. In order to address the wider issues affecting the community, opportunities are needed for:
- networking between reservation and urban ministries
- collaboration among leadership groups
- critical reflection in local, regional and national forums

These opportunities are especially needed in confronting significant justice issues faced by all: racism, poverty and cultural disintegration.

To a great degree, the minority experience in the church is an urban one. The majority of Native Americans are now urban, including most the 517 federally recognized tribes.[3] The preliminary 1990 census figures show that the largest Native American populations by census track designation are in three metropolitan areas, in order: Los Angeles, Tucson and New York. The three states with the largest Native American populations are, in order: Oklahoma, California and

Arizona.[4]

Much of the popularized awareness and knowledge of Native Americans is from the perspective of the reservation. This reality, so far removed from the mainstream of American life and consciousness, sustains a distorted view of the national community and the urgency of its needs and issues. What is true on the reservation is now also a reality in the city. Since Native Americans are seen as persons who do not live "next door," the stereotypes, prejudice and devaluation of their culture will continue. Worse, the culture can easily be idealized and made into an artifact to be consumed without connection to its spiritual foundation.

Although the reservation remains the locus for most of the Native American community in terms of social, religious and cultural identity, the majority find their economic future in or near the city. Less than one quarter of all Native Americans live on the reservation or trust lands.

However, the city is no promised land. Unemployment rates are 18% to 66% compared to 5.8% to 7.4% of the national average. The median income of Native Americans is only 50% of that for whites. Adolescent suicides have risen 1,000% over the past 20 years. Arrest rates are 10 times that of whites and three times that of African Americans. Drug and alcohol abuse is at twice the national average.[5]

This reality presents a unique opportunity for the church and its educational, human service and pastoral institutions to respond in innovative ways. Both the richness of Native American spirituality and the complexity of our cultural life need to be brought into the heart of the American Catholic Church experience. Unfortunately, our invisibility persists, based on the popular presumption that the Native American is safely tucked away and out of sight on the reservation. This perception affects the urban population, who do not have the social and political strength in numbers to force access to the means of addressing their poverty, addiction and familial disintegration.

> *We need to educate our Native people about the life of Kateri Tekakwitha and her love for God. We must keep struggling to find a place in the church.*
>
> **William Sunday**
> **Mohawk**
> **New York**

Urban Native American ministry is just beginning. It is, in many respects, a ministry to the "whirlwind." In the city, urban ministry attempts to grasp the extremes lived out by a mobile, young and intertribal community. Native Americans typically change addresses and jobs frequently, do not cluster in a "ghetto," have multiple agencies, if they are lucky, attempting to meet competing needs. More typically, they have no advocacy for the basics of survival in the urban community. In the larger urban centers many Native American organizations with limited resources vie for the support and involvement of the broad spectrum of people. Many are connected to an intertribal cultural community, many more are not.

Many newcomers are lost in the vast dark world of the inner city, and those who have assimilated into the middle and professional class are isolated in their own unique way. The urban community is desperately in search of a center out of which it can gather itself, strengthen and encourage one another toward the

future. The church can provide this opportunity in its ministry and presence to the community. The emerging directions for urban ministry can be summarized under the following components.

Outreach

The vast majority of urban Native Americans do not practice either a traditional or Christian religious life, individually or in community. This reality contributes to the stress and dysfunctionality expressed in addiction, physical and sexual abuse, depression, alienation and sucide. These are root experiences in urban life for too many, especially children and youth. Outreach is essential in breaking into this cycle and repeatedly inviting Native persons to belong to a community of faith and support. The many competing forces in urban life make it essential to develop communication, assessment, organization, collaboration and respect for differences.

Communication. Consistent and quality communication, either by newsletter, bulletin or advertisement, needs to be developed to reach both the Native American and Catholic communities. To reach the former, a mailing list can be gathered of persons and organizations through which to share the word about news, activities and plans.

Since many isolated Native Americans are part of our parishes, local leadership and fraternal organizations, communication is needed to this segment of the church. Also needed is an opportunity for advocacy and education, especially for pastoral leaders with no awareness of the Native American community.

Assessment. What is the shape of the community? What tribes and organizations are present and what needs are they meeting? Where do Native Americans gather? What needs are not being met by others? Assessment involves the Native American community, the Catholic community and civic institutions. Many Native organizations and leaders in the community have an educated sense of the community's history, present needs and emerging issues. These are invaluable in the proper assessment of the community. A balanced assessment of what is available to serve the community through the church and other social service programs provides good clues for short- and long-range goals. This assessment also can help to build the foundation for successful collaboration and the development of shared resources.

Community organizing. This aspect is the most difficult, due to the isolation and alienation felt by so many in urban life. The resistance to the unknown minister, and thus the ministry, can best be met with a commitment to consistent presence, listening, trust building and the invitation to share in the growing faith community.

Collaboration. Urban community organizing can be most effective when it is a collaborative effort between churches and social service agencies in common cause. This will require the development of resources for education and advocacy for the broad spectrum of the community.

Respect. Sensitive respect for tribal-specific differences must accompany

attempts to draw this richness into the life of the community and to provide opportunities for sharing traditional culture, significant factors in the development of a vibrant faith community. "Pan-Indian" or "intertribal" consciousness and cultural commonality are valuable contributions to communal identity and unity. However, a balance needs to be struck that does not undermine the tribal-specific richness. We are "Catholic Native Americans," but we are always "Lakota," "Chippewa," etc.

Pre-evangelization

The starting point for urban ministry is pre-evanglization. It creates support for the reclamation of self-identity, esteem and direction in an alien world. Both individuals and the community itself need to acquire the skills to meet the challenges of urban life and combat the psychological and spiritual resignation constitutive in assimilation.

An aware and concerned Native American community willing and able to support and encourage the learning of healthy life skills and the transmission of traditional values is essential. The Native American Christian community is unique in this regard. In fostering social and religious integrity the church is a path back to community, a way out of isolation and alienation, and a means for the reappropriation of one's unique culture. This community must be sustained in the tension felt in reflecting traditional values and reaching out to those individuals who need more.

Education

The role of education is a multidimensional and ongoing engagement for the Native American community and for the institutions of church and society. Ignorance and prejudice are too often the motivation for inaction. Through consistent education to the issues, needs and lived experience of all these entities, the goals of enculturation and inclusion will be realized.

Evangelization

In a related chapter this area is addressed in detail. It is important here to emphasize the centrality of the Gospel in the development of leadership and communal discernment. The process of the "de-colonialization" of the Gospel into contemporary Native American sensibility will course through the cycle of engaging the experience for both community and individual in breaking codependent behavior. The individual expresses this codependency in the lack of self-esteem, confidence, and responsibility for one's life and faith. Communal codependency is felt in the loss, anger, alienation from spiritual values, the land, family and tribe. This is engaging the experience of being a "victim" and confronting its effects.

Evangelization can be the experience of a shared discovery of self-reliance, renewed responsibility, connecting one's faith to the life of the community—in short, "re-membering." It is then more than awareness. It is action for the sake of others beyond oneself, i.e., the community and its future. The qualities of ministry and prophetic leadership have an opportunity to develop because of a freer imagination, enlightened by the Gospel, about oneself and one's place in the community.

Inclusion

Urban Native American ministry is itself multicultural, given the vast diversity of tribes and traditions that make up any sizable urban Native American community. Consideration of any authentic enculturation process must be based on the experience of inclusion, dialogue and consensus-based discernment in an intertribal world.

Outreach to the urban community is a ministry to the extremes. On the one side are those who are alienated and angry, searching and lost on the path for a reflection of their identity as Native Americans. On the other side are those "missionized" Native Americans who are quite comfortable with the traditional Catholic piety and liturgical expressions that have supplanted traditional life. In the middle are a vast number of unevangelized youth, young adults and families. Many are assimilated and, usually, interracial Native Americans with no connection to the community. Many follow the seasonal trail of "Pow-Wows" and seek out traditional ceremonial occasions to maintain an identity.

Urban ministry is challenged to address this spectrum and create opportunities for mutual support, interaction and, in the end, the development of a challenging experience of community. This process connects the city and the reservation experience. In creating this connection, an effective means of addressing the legal and cultural survival issues can be sustained. Further, a deeper consciousness about the life and death issues that confront the wider Native American community can enter a wider field of discussion and involvement. Often, knowledge of the most urgent issues affecting the Native American is outside mainstream media coverage, even in the church.

Participation

Urban ministry is a challenge to the church to be an active and prophetic participant in the life and issues that affect the wider Native American community in the urban complex. Those charged with leadership are called upon to create an effective presence of the church in the life of the urban community. Participation, where appropriate, can lend support in regard to civic and political issues affecting the community, and in ecumenical collaboration. It is also essential to be present to and empower the development of the social and cultural life of the urban community. The church's affirmation and understanding of the urban Native American can further an integration process that is sensitive and respectful.

Reculturation/Enculturation

Both the Native American community and the church are hard put at present to further the process of enculturation in the city. The process must grapple with the equally difficult question of "reculturation" of a large segment of the Native American population with little or no experience of traditional life and values. Tens of thousands of Native Americans have been born in the city over the last three decades. The Bureau of Indian Affairs' Relocation Program caused a cultural vacuum in an urban community. Most struggle with the pain and alienation inherent in assimilation. Far too many just give up. The present dilemma is one of addressing both the experience of the reservation, generally a monoculture,

and the urban multitribal reality.

A bridge must be built by the church and tribal organizations for the sake of cultural and religious survival. The strength of our cultural life and values needs to be transmitted to an emerging generation in the city who hunger for a sense of their own uniqueness. The next generation on the reservation needs to know, as well, the importance of acquiring self-esteem, self-reliance and effective life skills to move beyond just surviving.

Researchers have pointed out that three segments of the community experience being "Native American" differently. Each will have different answers about what is authentic, meaningful and important to preserve. Each brings with it a wealth of opportunity for the Native American community to access. Our own bias and anger keep us from engaging these experiences in the development of an integration of all expressions of our "Native ways" in the community.

Traditional. The traditional Native American is centered in the living out and caring for traditional cultural and spiritual values and rituals. Usually these are elders and those who have made a determined decision to remain within the reservation community or to practice traditional ways in the city. Youth and young adults are attempting to rediscover their traditional roots and to identify elders, medicine and ceremonial leaders to guide them.

Bicultural. Many in the city for any length of time must develop the capacity to deal successfully with the demands of urban life. Many of these same Native Americans are not willing to give up their roots in the cultural and spiritual life of the Native American community to survive. Maintaining relationships and extended family ties is central. Support for others who share in the struggle to hold onto their identity, culture and values is maintained with a view toward transmitting the culture to the next generation.

Assimilated. The Native American who has not been born, raised or, typically, has never returned to the reservation (or has no reservation) is confronted with the reality of assimilation. Many are second and third generation Native Americans "relocated" from the reservation. Many are interracial and intertribal in parentage, knowing that they have "Indian" bloodlines but lacking any real connection to a tribal or cultural experience. A growing segment of this population is searching for traditional values and identification and the qualities of life that can sustain them. Still others have no use for the tradition or all that is part of the dysfunctionality of the community.

Each of these segments of the urban community has unique needs, expectations and experiences of themselves that must be affirmed and engaged in urban ministry. Each is blessed with the capacity to inform, educate and lead in the renewal of the religious and cultural life of the community in a pastoral context. It is a question of how they can "bridge" their unique perspectives for something greater than themselves, that is, the future of the community.

We thus cannot speak of our youth without the essential connection with a fast-dying elder population that holds the wealth of tradition, language, song, dance, art and history. The bridge must be built with urgent deliberation.

From the Four Directions

Although many things can be said about the Native community as a whole, generalizations frequently obscure rather than clarify who the Native American is today. Regional and tribal-specific traditions, ceremony and history are valued treasures. These help to define and maintain individual and communal identity. This truth should not be underestimated in terms of the value and import for the community.

While unique tribal traditions aid in maintaining a cultural integrity, most Native Americans also see themselves as part of the larger whole. The awareness by the church of the unique diversity in its Native American sisters and brothers is critical in an urban environment where many tribal traditions are represented. Such awareness is also problematic, because no one methodology will serve the needs or wants of all. The good news is that by engaging this diverse community, the quality and richness of local church experience is potentially enhanced beyond what we can imagine.

Recommendations:
- **Leadership discernment**. Provide for an authentic involvement of the Native American community in the decision for selection and commissioning of lay leaders and in the discernment with individuals toward ordination.
- **Role of elders**. Affirm and support the role of the elders in parish and wider communal discernment for the care of the community.
- **Traditional forms**. Experiment with ecclesial structures and forms of church organization and leadership that respect the traditional social and cultural organization of the community.
- **Collaboration**. In urban areas with many tribal representations, foster a collaboration among the church, civic and nonprofit organizations in shaping the form and direction of ministry.

An Indigenous Christ?

The history of the relationship between the Catholic Church and the Native Americans in our hemisphere is well-documented, but essentially unknown. Either is it ignored, devalued or denied. In welcoming Pope John Paul II to Argentina, the indigenous people spoke these words that sound to the depths of their hearts the cost of the gift of faith.

> Welcome be Pope John Paul II, to the land that in its origins belonged to our ancestors and that today we no longer possess. On their behalf and ours, we that have survived the massacre and genocide...declare you guest and brother....
>
> We used to be free and the land, that is, our mother of the Native American, was ours. We lived from what she offered to us with generosity and everyone ate in abundance. Nobody lacked food....We used to praise our God in our language, with our gestures and dances, with instruments made by us. Until the day European civilization arrived. It erected the sword, the language and the cross and made us crucified nations. The Native American blood martyrized yesterday defending what was theirs, is the sea of the silenced martyrs of today. We, at a slow pace, are carrying the cross of five centuries. In this cross that they brought to America they changed the Christ of Judaea for the Indigenous Christ.[6]

A fundamental question is: Does the church perceive in its indigenous population this *indigenous Christ*? Some in church leadership have assumed that "assimilation" is the right and proper response to the inclusion of the Native American in church life. The unarticulated attitude is thus: "Enculturation may be worth trying but it won't really change things in the church." Many Native Americans view the church with bewilderment and experience pain in the unhealed memories of the past. Many are resentful at the continuing suppression by some church leaders of their language, spirituality, traditions, culture and ceremony. Some well-intentioned pastoral leadership sustains this experience out of ignorance and the fear of offending. Occasionally, this resistance masks a prejudice and rigidity when confronted with a culture so radically different from the dominate.

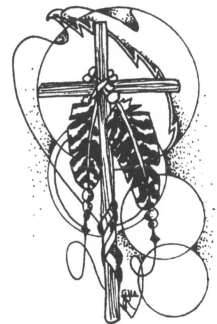

Training in issues related to multicultural ministry and cultural diversity is essential in the education and subsequent placement of pastoral leaders. The path from the margins to the center of church life is full of unanswered questions, unarticulated needs, tender sensibilities and unrealizable expectations. Each step along the way needs to be based on a shared responsibility for the last step taken and the one to come. The words of reconciliation must be marked repeatedly with positive action if a confidence is to be gained that both heals and empowers a broken community.

The statements about the Fifth Centenary year issued by the Catholic bishops and many Protestant groups have been received by the Native American community. Unvoiced questions often accompanies their reception: What changes can we expect? Is the church ready to deal with the breadth of Native American experience? Is the church capable of meeting the indigenous peoples on a common ground? These questions are just beginning to be addressed and there are signs of hope in the quality of response by the church leadership.

What has taken 25 generations to fracture, devalue and disempower will not be healed without patience, love and humility on the part of the national and local church. Nor will it be healed without the creation of a renewal process on the part of the Christian Native American community to move beyond grief over the past and into hope in the future. The Native American must understand the seeming slowness of the spiritual and political education of church leadership about the issues. In turn, the church leadership must be educated to the remarkable quality of immediacy felt in the Native American consciousness about these life issues. For both, it is a question of how to achieve a new consciousness about the meaning of the integration of spirituality, cultural and sociopolitical life.

The National Conference of Catholic Bishops in 1977 issued the *Statement of U.S. Catholic Bishops on American Indians* and, in response to the observance of the 500th anniversary of the evangelization of the Americas, the pastoral letter *Heritage and Hope: Evangelization in the United States*. Their message of reconciliation states:

It is our hope that during 1992 and thereafter, our nation will give special attention to the condition of Native Americans. We encourage all Americans to better understand the role of native peoples in our history and to respond to the just grievances of our Native American brothers and sisters....

We wish to strive for a new reconciliation in the spirit of the gospel among all Americans and to recognize more fully our solidarity with the nations of this hemisphere. Evangelization is unfinished if exploitation of the weak, of minorities, and of peoples of the third world countries still exists. The Quincentenary calls us to a new commitment as Christians to right the evils of the past and the present and to be forceful advocates of the peace and justice proclaimed by the gospel.[7]

It is essential for the church to believe that the Native American community is not just another "minority" among so many. The Native American community as a whole views itself as the "original" people of this land and thus prior to those who followed. The historical, social and cultural complexity of the national community demands a quality of recognition based on considerations that most Americans are not easily comfortable with, let alone understand. Many tribes believe the church has not understood or has ignored the fundamental Anglo-Saxon notion of sovereignty and "nationhood" as constitutive of tribal identity, even for Christian Native Americans.

The church has applied a generalized understanding of all ethnic and racial minorities as equal in ecclesial praxis. This cannot be successfully applied to Native Americans, who view themselves, by treaty and cultural distinction, as *nations within a nation*. Without respect, honor and dialogue with the social organization of the tribe, the church will always be outside, threatening the integrity of the whole. The pursuit of enculturation and opportunities for evangelization will always be divisive unless the church willingly engages the broader tribal reality as a distinct, sociocultural reality of worth and preservation that predates the arrival of Christianity in this hemisphere.

The multitude of Native American nations not only received the Gospel but welcomed with honor and respect those who brought such, without invitation, to their home and into the heart of their communal life. At this time, we only ask the same for ourselves. This diverse community of nations did not come to this continent because of religious, social, cultural or economic oppression; rather, they were the recipients thereof. The church misses an essential truth if it assumes without critical reflection that the Native American community is just another "minority" in competition for attention and proactive response. The church's apology, given now without action to redress the past and without a fundamental commitment toward a dignified future, would impoverish both the Native American and the possibility of reconciliation by this nation with its own history.

Our prophetic witness to the church is to challenge it to share with us in the struggle to shape a national conscience, based both on the Gospel and on our interdependent experience of spirituality, sociopolitical life and ecology.

In this time of reflection on the Columbus event, the World Council of Churches, the National Council of Churches and such American denominations as the Presbyterian Church (USA) and the United Church of Christ have made it a priority to confront the past and attempt to create a new relationship with indigenous peoples. All those engaged in leadership in both in the Native American community and in the ministry of the church are thus challenged to chart the new path and be prophetic witnesses within the Christian churches.

The National Council of Churches resolution of May 1990, for example, expressed the following:

> ...therefore, it is appropriate for the Church to reflect on its role in that historical tragedy; to repent of its complicity and, in pursuing a healing process, to move forward in our witness for justice and peace.[8]

Reconciliation is, as the Apostle Paul states, a ministry of all Christians. The call of the United States Catholic bishops for reconciliation and advocacy for justice needs to be heard in the halls of all our institutions and to be constitutive in all our programs, if we as a people are to be understood for who we truly were in the past for the sake of future generations.

Recommendations:
- **Urban ministry.** Develop urban ministry for the Native American community in those dioceses where significant numbers of Native Americans now live.
- **Education of clergy and lay leadership.** As part of their pastoral formation, educate church leadership at all levels about the essential issues which confront the Native American community and about the richness of the traditions.
- **Ad hoc committee.** Establish an ad hoc committee in the National Conference of Catholic Bishops to provide the social, theological and political analysis necessary in addressing the needs of the Native American population.
- **Advocacy.** Include in the national agenda of all Catholic organizations an assessment of their policies that constructively involve Native American issues and needs.

The average Native American has little understanding of the Christian churches' historical divisions, among themselves, of the Native American territory. Without consultation or consideration of the impact on the dignity of our collective life, they divided the Native American soul. We now ask that these same churches engage one another in reconstituting the future of the people. The collaboration, advocacy and mutual support of the churches is vital on the reservation and in the city for the advancement of the Native American community.

In the face of persistent cuts in federal and state funding for Native American programs, the church is now the moral and, in many cases, the financial mainstay in the Native communities for advocacy for religious freedom, legal redress on land claims and the support of schools, clinics and the like. Collaboration needs to be developed on a national level to enhance the effectiveness of advocacy for the rights of the Native American to the federal and state governments. Without aggressive and persistent commitment to this role, the churches will continue to journey parallel paths and thus lessen their capacity to effectively impact the future of the Native American community as a whole.

Recommendations:
- **Dialogue.** Establish inter-church dialogue on the theological, liturgical and pastoral enculturation of Native American traditions for both reservation and urban populations.
- **Mutual support.** Provide collaboration among the churches involved in ministries with Native Americans, both on the reservation and in the city, in order to share resources and to plan pastoral and lay leadership formation.

Silent Racism

The tragedy of our collective past—and present—is the ignorance and racism that in many ways fosters public policy, and the private silence that results in ongoing destruction of the Native American life and culture. To understand the condition of the Native American today is to confront the continuing racism and denial of basic human rights and thus to admit a history of social, economic and political exploitation.

The Racial Ethnic Task Force of the 200th General Assembly of the Presbyterian Church (USA) defined racism as "any self-perpetuating, systematic, and sustained use of power by one ethnic group over another."[9] In concluding their report, they state the following:

> From the beginning, the experience of racial ethnic people within the United States has been one of racism, with racial violence but one manifestation of the deep abiding sin which permeates our society. This racism undergirds a systematic economic exploitation of people of color which benefits White America....Native American Nations suffered systematic removal from valuable land coveted by European immigrants, the breaking of all legitimate treaties, and the wholesale destruction of their populations and cultures. They were confined and banished to reservations, sometimes distant from ancestral homes, or to a marginal existence in cities where their small numbers makes them one of the least visible of racial ethnic groups.[10]

Native American and Catholic

Are we Native American or are we Catholic? Which is first, which follows? How do we choose? An even more fundamental and difficult question arises: Does the Native American community need the church at this time in its history to meet fundamental needs and to recreate itself?

Many Christian Native Americans do not find that being Native American and being Christian is a choice that the Lord asks or even wants us to make. The Native American can and does live effectively with both realities due to our spirituality and collective psychology which are not based on Western categorical models. For the youth, the majority of the national population, the struggle for identity and self-esteem does, however, create an almost irreconcilable division. Many are returning to traditional practices in an attempt to counter assimilation. In this regard, the church is not adequately equipped to provide the means for re-culturation or an engaging experience of an enculturated Christian Native American faith community, especially off the reservation. Where urban ministries have been established, however, valid and meaningful inroads are being made to touch this significant part of the community.

We do know that the heart and soul of the Native American has not yet been put into the language and ritual of Christian faith. This is the challenge we bring to the church—to seek out a grammar of assent together. The challenge is to explore imaginatively new models and methods of leadership and decision making, as well as religious education and ministry formation that respect and honor the fundamental social and spiritual dynamics that hold Native communities together.

The invitation to participate in this process must be to the holders of our traditional and cultural life—the elders, the medicine people, the ceremonial leaders, the story tellers, the artists and the singers. This can only be accomplished by creating a level of trust and confidence that the integrity of our culture and history can be transmitted intact within a Christian context. So far this has not been demonstrated effectively. This part of the work is not ours, but the church's.

The challenge is urgent. Within perhaps the next generation, many of our elders will be gone and, with them, the connection to a thousand generations past.

The indigenous peoples of North and South America have now wandered in their unique subjugation more than five generations longer than the sojourn of Israel in Egypt and we, too, have a sacred story to tell. We invite the church to listen. Listening to this story is perhaps the most significant and difficult initial step in the process of healing and interdependence, and particularly difficult for the Eurocentric church that is used to an institutional model of church governance and practice.

The challenge is one of conversion from a patriarchic and hierarchic self-formation to that of the circle, with its understood equality of presence, engagement and responsibility for the whole. This challenge to formulate a prophetic social justice agenda is fundamentally "American" and elemental to the emergence of an authentic enculturated American Christian spirituality. To engage the wealth of the Native American tradition will allow for no less and can imagine far more.

It is to learn from the vision quest, that journey into the unknown where we meet our angels and devils and find a new purpose, hope and name. It is to trust the sweat lodge, the kiva, the talking circle, the medicine wheel—all those rites of healing renewal.

Where the traditions and culture are strong, the church can learn from the story of the people and from their expression of the sacred manner in which they live. Where the traditions and culture are weak, the church can offer their best by investing in—with minds, hands and dollars—the reclamation of the culture by the people themselves. The conditions for an enculturated spirituality, worship and sacramental life need to be based on an acceptance of the cornerstones of Native American life: rites of passage, the role of elders and women, extended family and communal responsibility for the appropriate development of the individual. These conditions can and do inform the institutional model of church and the pastoral response it makes toward children, youth, young adults, family and elders for the sake of our traditions. These we will not let go.

Being a member of one of the oldest tribes in the Southwest has enlightened my spirit. I feel closely identified with nature. That feeling shortens the path to the Almighty, giving my soul the peaceful environment that creates meaning in life.

Connie Torrez
Tigua Indian Community
El Paso, Texas

Reclamation of the Sacred

Our challenge to the church is to invite the Native American into a full maturity and dignity within the church, with our unique and treasured traditions, spirituality and languages intact and honored. Inviting our specific cultural pluralism and diversity into the church, along with our many languages, representing hundreds of living tribal heritages, is a tremendous task that will require scholarship from the church. Much of the work in this process needs to be done by our Native leadership and the people themselves, but without the dedication of the church in inviting this grassroots development process, it will not happen. The proverbial presence of the anthropologist, sociologist and psychologist in the cultural life of the Native American community cannot replace the role of the church in the reclamation of the sacred and its appropriate inclusion in the life of the whole.

Recommendations:
- **Consultation.** Establish a forum for spirituality and worship for Native American and pastoral ministry leadership from both the reservation and urban church.
- **Models.** Explore models of leadership, decision making and ministry, based on traditional Native American social, political and religious organization.
- **Cultural advocacy.** Support and encourage the appropriate educational and cultural institutions in the church in preserving and enhancing tribal traditions, culture and language, and use these in religious education, ministry formation and lay leadership development for both Native Americans and non-Indians alike.

Finding the Power

Ironically, North American Native Americans are one of the most institution-alized ethnic and racial populations in the world. From the government schools, hospitals, clinics, training programs, jails and federal-funded service centers to the church-funded institutions of all descriptions, Native Americans have had historically little or no input into the very institutions mandated to assist them. This has left the community with little motivation, sense of self, communal determination or investment in the future. The cycle can be broken by inviting, supporting and training Native Americans on a broad scale to assume leadership for their own. This has happened in many Christian and Roman Catholic missions, schools and programs across the country. More needs to be done.

Recommendations:
- **Restoring the path.** Provide models of leadership and decision making based on traditional tribal organization and practice, especially in matriarchical societies.
- **Discernment.** Create structures for community-based discernment of present and future needs of the community and indigenous methods for addressing these.
- **Traditional education.** Affirm the role of elders and tradition keepers and enhance support for new generations to be educated in the tribal traditions and culture.

The New Wisdom-Keepers

According to the U.S. Department of Health and Human Services in 1988, an estimated 400,000 Native Americans are under the age of 15. The median ages are 20 for American Native Americans and 18 for Alaska Natives; the national average is 30. The context for considering educational issues and Native Americans are complex. In the study *American Native American Children and Adolescents,* the authors summarize the current condition of education:

> About one-third of adult American Native Americans are classified as illiterate, and only one adult male in five has a high school education (Brod and McQuiston, 1983). Dropout rates in urban high schools are particularly high, sometimes reaching 85%. In reservation schools and in boarding schools, which together educate about 80% of Native American youth, approximately 50% drop out (Coladarci, 1983; Giles, 1985).
>
> The dearth of college-educated American Native Americans (8% according to U.S. Bureau of the Census, 1984) has substantial impact on this population. At the graduate level, the under-representation of American Native Americans is even more dramatic....Of the 32,839 doctoral degrees awarded in 1987 nationwide, only 130 were to American Native Americans, and only 10 of those were in psychology. Without psychologists, social workers, psychiatrists, and researchers who are sensitive to the complexity of American Native American cultural values, tribal customs, family ecology, and communications styles, collaboration and service delivery with American Native Americans will continue to be ineffective.[11]

Calling Forth a New Generation

The role of national associations of professional educators, human service and pastoral ministry professionals in relation to the Native American community past and present is twofold. First and foremost, the urgent need is for outreach, both on the reservation and in the city, to gain access to the best our educational and professional institutions can offer.

Recommendations:
- **Affirmative action.** Take affirmation action in the recruitment of qualified Native Americans and support the mentoring required for the appropriation of the skills necessary to be effective professionals.
- **Training.** Provide cross-cultural training both for Native Americans and others interested in the advancement of the Native American community both on the reservation and in the city; also provide opportunities for Native Americans to gain access to a broader base of experience and professional expectations.
- **Collaboration.** Promote collaboration among organizations in the development of funding, programs and resources for the benefit of the Native American community and for the wider development of the culture. This collaboration would include tribal leadership and programs both on the reservation and in the city.

Reliable statistics on the number of Native American students in Catholic elementary, middle, secondary and college institutions are difficult to obtain. The vast majority of Native Americans have mixed bloodlines, either with non-Indian parentage or with Native Americans of other tribes. Many are not registered members of their respective tribes as a result of mixed parentage or because of legal restrictions imposed both by tribes and the federal government. As a result,

grants, scholarships and financial aid mandated for Native Americans are not readily accessible. Many are reluctant to self-identify as Native American out of shame, shyness or ignorance. Many are assumed to be Latino or Hispanic on the basis of skin color, surname or interracial parentage.

The major role of professional educators must be in the transmission of the reality of the Native American experience in North America. So many times the mythic images of the "noble savage" or the grand battles of the Western expansion are the only information passed to the next generation in American textbooks, written from a Eurocentric perspective. The Native American perspective is rarely presented except as indigenous contributions to the national trust in academic specialties in history, civics/law, ecology, art, medicine, agriculture, psychology and religion. Multiculturalism in education and civic life does not deal with the problematic. The multicultural reality and, in particular, the tribal-specific tradition of our people has always been in the background, undervalued but resistant to the ill-founded "American" myth of monoculturalism (the proverbial "melting pot").

Recommendations:
- **Review.** Develop a review committee of educators, publishers, scholars and Native American leaders to review textbooks and curriculum about the Fifth Centenary and the quality of education relative to Native American life, culture, tradition and spirituality taught at all levels of our educational system.
- **Education.** Support and encourage the formation of standing committees within existing professional associations to assess the quality of educational programs, especially in regard to the use of racially or culturally biased testing instruments for Native American youth.
- **Assessment.** Encourage educational and professional organizations to make access, recruitment and support for Native American advancement a priority now and in the years to come.

Religious Education

The role of religious education at the local level is one of the most important links to the Native American community, both on and off the reservation. Of special interest is the recognition of Native American students and their families, especially in their sacramental and spiritual formation. At these pivotal moments we can make the most authentic and appropriate connections between traditional rites of passage and the church's sacramental system. Administrators at diocesan, regional and local parish levels must be aware of the significance of these moments within the life of the Native American child.

At best, these sacramental moments are parallelled within the Native American tradition but, unfortunately, have no connection to the life of the parish or education program. At worst, the Native American family is not connected to the urban Native American community, and thus forsakes traditional rites. Many times families feel impoverished by the experience.

Recommendations:
- **National responsibility.** As staff in the national offices of religious education, youth and young adult ministry and campus ministry, participate proactively in the outreach to Native Americans in the life of the local church.

● **New methods.** Develop the theological and pastoral reflection necessary for effective ministerial strategies to multicultural and indigenous populations.

The Sacred Home

The impact of the sudden conjunction of two vastly different cultures that began 500 years ago is felt by the indigenous peoples of this hemisphere to this very day. We are in a critical time as a nation. The truth of the Native American experience confronts our national myths and illusions about ourselves. For many, this reality creates not only resistance but also a pain that will not go away. It is the pain of a people who will not go away, of a history that has not been taught, and of a present reality that questions the very values upon which we declare ourselves a nation of compassion and justice. Kirkpatrick Sale states the dilemma thus:

> Everything of importance in the succeeding 500 years stems from that momentous event: the rise of Europe, the triumph of capitalism, the creation of the nation state, the dominance of science, the establishment of a global monoculture, the genocide of the indigenous, the slavery of people of color, the colonialization of the world, the destruction of primal environments, the eradication and abuse of species and the impending catastrophe of ecocide for the planet earth.
>
> For the future, there is only one lesson: The only political vision that offers any hope of salvation, one based on an understanding of, a rootedness in, a deep commitment to, and a resacralization of, place....Such a politics, based, as the original peoples of the America's had it, upon love of place, also implies the place of love. For ultimately love is the true cradle of politics, the love of the earth and its systems, the love of the particular bioregion we inhabit, the love of those who share it with us in our communities, and the love of that unnameable essence that binds us together with the earth, and provides the water for the roots we sink.[12]

The pain of the Native American comes from the disconnection with the land. Yet is also a pain transformed by a love that is remembered, a love hoped for because we need the love of place to define us as one people. It is a love of the Creator and the Lord that will enable us to be transformed by our pain and our unresolved past into a church that is capable of meeting an Indigenous Christ in us.

Notes

1. A quote from the "Journal of Christopher Columbus" in H. Zinn, *A People's History of the United States*, New York, Harper Colophon Books, Harper and Row, 1980.

2. Luis N. Rivera-Pagan, "A New World and a New Church: The Discovery and Conquest of America as an Imperial Missionary Enterprise," presented at the Cross Caucus, Presbyterian Church (U.S.A.), San Juan, PR, 1990.

3. The federal government recognizes 517 native entities: 196 in Alaska and 321 in lower states and 36 state-recognized tribes. Demographic data cited in J. T. Gibbs and L. N. Huang, eds., *Children of Color: Psychological Interventions with Minority Youth*, San Francisco, CA, Jossey-Bass, 1989, pp. 115f.

4. Summary of 1990 census figures from the *U.S. Department of Commerce News*, Washington, DC, Department of Commerce, Summer 1991.

5. T.D. LaFromboise and K. Grafflow, op. cit.

6. Message to Pope John Paul by the Indians of Argentina, cited in L.N. Rivera-Pagan, op. cit.

7. *Heritage and Hope: Evangelization in the United States,* Washington, DC, National Conference of Catholic Bishops, November 1990, pp. 42-43.

8. National Council of Churches (USA) Resolution, May 1990.

9. Racial Ethnic Task Force, 200th General Assembly, Presbyterian Church (U.S.A.), Houston, TX, May 1990.

10. Ibid.

11. T. D. LaFromboise and K. G. Grafflow, op. cit.

12. Kirkpatrick Sale, "What Columbus Discovered," *The Nation,* October 22, 1990, pp. 444 ff.

CHAPTER VII

PRACTICAL HELPS FOR TEACHERS

O ur first task in approaching
another people
another culture
another religion
is to take off our shoes
for the place we are
approaching is holy.
Else we may find ourselves
treading on another's
dream. More serious
still, we may forget...
that God
was there before our arrival.

Guidelines for Cultural Sensitivity with Native Americans

North American society provides a multicultural context for the experience of the Roman Catholic Church.
- Assimilation is no longer the guiding principle among the various racial, ethnic and national groups in our society.
- The preservation and practice of one's own culture, traditions and languages

are of primary value.

- North American society is a blend of various groups: each maintaining its own identity while producing a North American tapestry.
- Native Americans hold a unique place in this tapestry as the original inhabitants of this land.
- While Native Americans are a minority, their cultures, languages and traditions have equal value with other racial/ethnic groups in a multicultural society.

The value and integrity of all racial, ethnic and cultural groups must be respected. North American society is not the assimilation of all groups into one, but the experience of a community of communities.

Native Americans are diverse in their own cultures and traditions.
- The primary identification of Native Americans is with their village, tribe or nation.
- North of the Rio Grande, there are over 300 extant Native languages and cultures.
- The cultural differences among Native Americans are as diverse as among other cultural groups, such as Asians and Europeans.

Native peoples must be viewed through their own cultural tapestry. Programs must avoid an attempt to present a monocultural understanding of Native Americans.

Native Americans have had a variety of experiences of European contact.
- Some Native Americans had their initial European contact almost 500 years ago. Others have had substantial contact only in the last 150 years.
- The experience of European contact varied, partially because of the different European groups (English, French, Spanish, Russian) and their different approaches to colonization.
- A number of Native American peoples had their primary European contacts with Americans of European descent who no longer considered themselves to be immigrants.
- The experience of initial conversion to Catholic Christianity ranges from over 400 years to less than 100 years.

The variety of Native American histories with Europeans needs to be taken into account in programs and policies.

Native Americans have a diversity of experiences of living in a multicultural society.
- Some Native Americans live among their own people on their own land (reservations).
- Some Native Americans have grown up on their reservations and have migrated to an urban setting. For most, this is a real and dramatic experience of immigration.
- Many urban Native Americans (who constitute at least half of the Native population) maintain some contact with their cultures through Native centers and/or visits to their reservations.
- In urban areas, there will be Native Americans who are native to the area

and others who have migrated there from other parts of North America.
- Not all Native Americans have reservations. Some urban Natives belong to landless tribes. Their primary community is the multicultural urban experience of North American society.

The variety of reasons why Native Americans live where they do in our society needs to be understood and appreciated. Programs need to reflect their pluralistic experience.

Native Americans have a variety of experiences in regard to their own culture and to the dominant North American culture.
- After European contact, a number of Native American tribes lost their cultures and languages through the destruction of their villages. Some tribes disappeared while others continued with a few survivors.
- Through the experience of Christian missionization, some Native Americans lost their own culture and language and adopted European ones.
- Some Native Americans maintained two strictly divided cultural lives: one for the village or reservation and the other for the larger society and often for the church.
- Some Native Americans lost their culture and language because of the governmental assimilation efforts of previous years.
- Presently, a revival of Native cultures, traditions and languages is occurring. Many are regaining their culture.

The many diverse ways in which Native Americans relate to their own societies and to North American society must be appreciated in any program.

Native Americans continue to experience racial stereotyping and racism.
- Through centuries of contact, certain stereotypes have developed around Native Americans. The media has played a significant role in dispersing and supporting these stereotypes.
- Native Americans experience among themselves various forms of racism through tribal prejudices.
- Due to the experience of reservations, Native peoples have known the experience of forced segragation. The reservation system developed as a consequence of the Native people being a conquered people.
- Some Native Americans mistrust the institutions of the dominant culture, e.g., governmental agencies, church.

The reality of centuries of prejudice, racial stereotypes and racism needs to be acknowledged. Programs need to develop and support trusting relationships between Native Americans and the larger North American society.

Among Native Americans, the understanding of relationships provides some shared elements, as well as a means to embrace them in a pluralistic society.
- Native Americans arrive at their self-identity through the various relationships in which they share.
- How Native Americans experience these primary relationships will help in understanding a particular group. These relationships are with word, time, land and all creatures.

- Native Americans view themselves as living through these relationships in a sacred and spiritual world.

Programs need to appreciate the deeply spiritual world of Native Americans. An understanding of Native peoples' primary relationship will be of help in this area.

Native Americans experience relationships through words.
- The spoken word has a higher value than the written word. The use of story has primary importance; through the telling of one's tribe's stories, the people are given and sustained in life.
- The speaker's personal integrity gives credence and value to the words he or she speaks.
- The value of words lessens with their quantity. Some Native Americans may appear reticent when, in fact, they are respecting the value of the conversation.
- Silence has an intrinsic value. It is important to spend time in silence with people.

Any program must appreciate the Native relationship with word and must rely more on the spoken word than on the written word.

Native Americans experience relationships with time.
- The primary understanding of time is how it relates to the days, months, seasons of the world. Time is the expression of one's unity and harmony with the world.
- While the understanding of time by hours and minutes used in the dominant society has importance, it is secondary to the Native understanding of time.
- Through the use of ritual, one can place oneself in greater harmony with the rhythm of the world. History is not seen as linear but rather as cyclical; it reflects the movement of the world, of the seasons.
- Through respect for one's elders, this appreciation of one's history is reflected. The elders carry in their bodies the traditions and values of the people.

The Native understanding of time needs to be appreciated to avoid confusion. History is not viewed as a chronicle of past events but rather a reflection of living with the universe.

Native Americans experience relationships with the land.
- Native Americans view the world on which we live as mother earth, the giver and sustainer of our life.
- The land has a unique relationship with Native peoples. The sense of ownership differs. Native people do not "own" the land, but they and the land belong to one another.
- Native Americans view their relationship with the land as characterized by care, for our mother earth makes us who we are.

The unique Native relationship with the land needs to be reflected in any program. This relationship is characterized by mutual love and respect.

Native Americans experience relationships with all living creatures.

- All life is sacred and shared by all living creatures.
- No one form of life has a greater intrinsic value than another since all creatures form one family and share one common life.
- By living in harmony with all creatures, humans can live the life for which the Creator made them.

The Native understanding of life needs to be reflected in programs. The Creator's creatures share a common life.

Native Americans have a diverse cultural experience which is deeply spiritual.
- Native American culture is a spiritual one.
- In the faith expression of Native Americans, Catholic Christianity needs to be enculturated in the Native traditions and cultures. Otherwise, the adoption of Catholic Christianity would mean the loss of one's culture.
- Native spirituality and Catholic Christianity are compatible with one another.

Catholic Christianity needs to be enculturated in the various Native traditions and cultures, which are deeply spiritual. Such an approach reflects the acceptance of the pluralistic world in which we live.

Pedagogical Way of Entering Into and Sharing Native American Cultures

Use oral tradition, primarily storytelling, as the vehicle of instruction. This is a natural, exciting and memorable way.

Experience realities through personal presence in the family, tribe and scared ceremonies as the ordinary manner of learning. This is the best way to come to know the people and to form friendships.

Understand that traditional ways require leaders to give instructions. These leaders will let one know what and when to do things.

Respect older people teaching younger people. This is countercultural but needs to be maintained and restored.

Know that every culture has its etiquette in communication. It is necessary to know and respect the differences.

Take advantage of clear pictorial expressions which communicate best. Abstractions and theory may cloud the teachings.

Remember Native peoples live in a close relationship with the Creator. A religion of words alone is foreign to the people.

Catechize in such a way as to reflect the values, traditions and customs of the tribes. This comes easily out of gospel values.

Take time to listen to the elders (men and women) of the tribes to relearn, rediscover, reinforce their values. These are strengths which will be handed down

to the next generation.

Seek out the tribes' storytellers and learn their history, traditions and customs. This is a source of pride for the people.

Study and pray the Scriptures. This deepens the faith experience in relation to tribal history.

Explore spiritual insights God has given to the tribes. Ask what Christian teachings can be added or developed.

Integrate cultural values into religious education programs. This catechesis offers new experiences for the tribes as well as for the missionaries.

Turn to the gifts of creation as easy meditation for tribal people. Use them as tools for family gatherings.

Stress and affirm the following Native traditions. Awake to creation, reverence, respect, generosity. Challenge what seems to deny the best in them: harshness toward and neglect of children, choosing the way of noise and speed, and not passing on the most sacred values. This affirmation has helped others to be sensitive and to listen, no matter what the environment. This will make it possible for catechesis to happen.

Suggestions for a Native American Liturgy

- Conduct in the language and culture of the people.
- Base on the seasons and events important to the life of the people.
- Incorporate Native American symbolism, art and music in a meaningful way.
- Freely express their own faith in God.
- Celebrate the community's love for the Creator.
- Involve diverse forms for differing occasions.
- Include an intertribal sharing or liturgical experiences and experiments.
- Promote total Native American participation in preparation and planning of liturgies.
- Incorporate Native American prayer forms and customs approved by the people.
- Come from a catechized people (elders, etc.).
- Call for additional ministerial roles and affirm the gifts of the people.
- Express the identity of the people in Christ.
- Stress preaching (homilies) that forms the people in the Word of God.
- Clearly identify with Catholic worship.
- Allow for spontaneity.

Helps with Symbols and Sacred Ceremonies

The Native American world is one of meaningful symbols which help to encounter God, Creator, Great Spirit. Symbols and ceremonies express and present meaning which helps to provide purpose and understanding in the lives of human beings.

Symbols

The sacred circle is a symbol of wholeness and unity, establishing harmony and oneness with the earth, all of creation, humanity and the infinity of God. The circular design of some traditional dwellings, such as the tepee and sweatlodge, helps one to better understand life's journey for greater harmony during various stages of human growth and development.

The sacred drum and its beat is for many tribes the rhythmic beat of the human heart.

The medicine wheel helps one to visualize and understand ideas that cannot be seen. It shows the different ways all things of life are interconnected. The medicine wheel can show what the person is now (today) and what that person can become. When openness and motivation are present, one's potential begins to develop wholistically and leads the person to a real harmony of growth using all the gifts of creation as teachers. This sacred wheel (circle) is a medicine for a whole and healthy life. The sacred number "4" is very significant with this symbol. The medicine wheel to wholeness uses the 4 directions or grandfathers, 4 elements, 4 life forms, 4 areas of growth for the human person, 4 human needs and 4 growth processes for development as a person.

Dances use the circle as a sign of unity, strength and wholeness.

Sacred animals and birds are relatives, teachers and models that call forth further growth in life's journey.

Sacred plants such as sweetgrass, tobacco, cedar, sage, juniper and others designated by tribes, are burned for purification, healing, strength, wholeness and greater harmony in one's life.

Sacred rituals use sacred plants, elements which are nonrational but intuitive, and gestures which touch deep energy and release grace and energy for an individual or a group.

The hoop dance is symbolic of the earth and the moon. The gifted dancer uses about 28 hoops. The observer can even begin to feel the power and the life as the hoops are twirled and move on the arms, legs, neck and body of the dancer. As the dance continues, various formations of creation can be depicted to express the close relationship with God's creation.

Sacred Ceremonies

These ceremonies help some Native American tribal groups to keep life in balance, in harmony. They provide for spiritual knowledge and growth in order to be more rooted to the earth: "To know who I am and what I am."

The sacred pipe expresses the connectedness of the earth with the Creator. The pipe is filled with tobacco in a ritualistic fashion by offering the sacred plant in each of six directions or grandfathers (East, South, West, North, Sky and Earth) by the pipe carrier. Then it is smoked by the men gathered if it is a man's pipe, by women if it is a woman's pipe, and by both men and women if the pipe is to be used by both sexes. A sacred pipe is given when "earned" or handed on by an elder pipe carrier. This person has a special office or role within the tribal community and must live a lifestyle worthy of the title: sacred pipe carrier. The sacred pipe is also used in a sweatlodge, and with the sun dance and vision quest.

The sweatlodge is a purification rite for the spiritual, physical and mental health of a person. The lodge is made of willows, each one placed with a prayer. An animal skin covers the structure. The floor is covered with sage or cedar for healing. Hot rocks are placed in the center pit of the lodge to represent the six powers of the universe. Water sprinkled on the rocks is used to purify. The "sweat" is a time of prayer for spiritual direction in decision making or for greater strength in daily struggles.

The person who leads a "sweat," called a "sweatholder," conducts prayer by singing songs or chants as drumming is done. The sweatholder, who is also a sacred pipe carrier, will lead the group with the smoking of the sacred pipe. This rite is a powerful way to pray, discern, seek guidance and be strengthened.

The sundance is a ceremony of self-sacrifice for spiritual strength for the people and for the individual chosen to do a sundance. The ceremonial ground is specially constructed. A cottonwood tree is placed at the center with one cord per dancer tied at the top of the tree (pole) to be used on the fourth day for the piercing. The sundance begins a long preparation period, followed by four days and nights of fasting so that a person begins to change his/her life, to receive spiritual strength. Sage, used for purifying, healing and strength, is worn around the ankles and as a crown on the head. The dancers also blow a shrill whistle made of willow or eagle bone while the sundance is taking place. Also, the women (wives or close family members) dance and pray in the outer circle in support of and for strength for the men doing the sundance. On the fourth day, the sundancers are pierced on the left side of their chests and are attached to the cord of the pole at the center.

The dancers move toward the center and then back to the outer circle to the steady drum beat, each blowing the shrill whistle as he tries to break loose from the pole. When each is spiritually right, the pulling away happens and the dancer gives both flesh and blood for the people.

The vision quest is a four day and night fast alone on a hilltop in prayer. It is a time to listen to the voice of the Spirit in silence. The sacred pipe is held, linking the person to the earth while praying and/or crying out for a vision or powers needed to live in harmony with the world and to experience new life.

Blessed Kateri Tekakwitha
"I have called you by name..." (Isaiah 43:1)
"Come with me." (Matthew 4:19)

A little girl, named Tekakwitha by her family and tribal members of the Mohawk village, was born a Mohawk-Algonquin Native in 1656. As the result of a devastating smallpox epidemic, she was left orphaned and physically frail at the age of 4.

Despite Tekakwitha's losses during her early life, she appeared to have desired a strong and healthy relationship with the Creator (ne son kwa iat te son), God of the Christian Blackrobes, unknown to her uncle and aunt, her adopted parents.

As a member of the turtle clan, one of the main Mohawk clans, Tekakwitha lived a spirituality of her sacred animal from an early age. Just as a turtle moves straight ahead and is not hindered by any obstacles, she lived her name Tekakwitha (sometimes translated as moving all before her) by overcoming many stumbling blocks so that she could know the God of the Blackrobes better.

Like her sacred animal spirit, the turtle, Tekakwitha was close to mother earth. The rhythmic heartbeat of the land, where new life comes forth, sustained her as she daily walked in harmony with nature, with creation and with the Creator. Like the turtle that gently and in close relationship with the land moves deliberately and enjoys and learns from the whole of creation, Tekakwitha lived and walked in harmony with nature and her Creator.

As a young woman, she had strong and deep convictions. She dared to challenge some Iroquoian tribal values in order to pursue her goal. At the age of 20, she was baptized and was given the name Kateri (Catherine). Kateri Tekakwitha was a person of strength, dignity and hope. She walked the sacred circle of wholeness and desired fullness of life with the Creator God.

As a faithful follower of Christ, Kateri showed much determination and conviction in her journey to deepen a relationship with the Creator God for whom she daily hungered and thirsted. Jesus made a difference in her life. Her drum beat of life became much clearer and in harmony with her desires and hope that Christ Jesus be the center of her life.

Rome recognized Kateri as a special follower and declared her Venerable in 1943; in 1980, she became Blessed. Today, many Native American Catholics see Blessed Kateri Tekakwitha as one who continues to be in close relationship with her people as a role model, and one who was able to live out a controversial lifestyle in order to respond to a radical and passionate call to follow Christ.

Four Prayer Services

I.

Opening Song: *Holy Spirit* or another appropriate hymn
Response: "Spirit of our Maker" (alternate sides)

1. Spirit of our Maker,
Thank you for your blessings,
Hear your humble children.

Spirit of our Maker

2. Spirit of the Eagle,
Take our prayers to heaven,
Bring our Maker's blessings.

Spirit of our Maker
Spirit of the Eagle

3. Spirit of the Turtle,
Kateri, our sister,
Make us one in spirit.

Spirit of our Maker
Spirit of the Eagle
Spirit of the Turtle

4. Spirit of the Blackbird,
Red, white, black and yellow,
Bring us all together.

Spirit of our Maker
Spirit of the Eagle
Spirit of the Turtle
Spirit of the Blackbird

5. Spirit of our Mother,
Shelter us and feed us,
Comfort us and clothe us.

Spirit of our Maker
Spirit of the Eagle
Spirit of the Turtle
Spirit of the Blackbird
Spirit of our Mother

6. Spirit of our Savior,
Mercy and compassion,
Love for all your people.

Spirit of our Maker
Spirit of the Eagle
Spirit of the Turtle
Spirit of the Blackbird
Spirit of our Mother
Spirit of our Savior

7. Spirit of our Maker,
Honor, thanks, and glory,
Be to you forever.

Spirit of our Maker
Spirit of the Eagle
Spirit of the Turtle
Spirit of the Blackbird
Spirit of the Mother
Spirit of the Savior
Spirit of the Maker

Prayers of the Faithful
Respond "Lord, hear our prayer" to the petitions offered.

The Lord's Prayer

The Sign of Peace
(Permission by Great Spirit Congregation, Milwaukee, WI)

II.

Opening Prayer to the Great Creator and Maker
Help us to walk straight the
sacred path of life. Hearing
your voice and seeing
your beauty in creation
and creatures alike.

Give us the strength and
courage, our creator, to
perceive the sacredness
of life, of mother earth,
and of all creation.

Give us the vision to see
and admire your beautiful
creation.

Prayer Facing East
O Creator God, maker of all that is,
who always has been,
may the rising sun remind us of you

who gives us great wisdom and
strength. Help us your people
as we walk your sacred path
and life, so that our generations
to come will have light as
they walk your path.
For the rays of the rising sun
in the East,
We thank you, Our Creator.

Prayer Facing South
O Good Creator,
You send us soft winds and
rains from the South.
May goodness be always in
our hearts and gentleness
in our speech.
We are reminded of the
things that make us
happy in this life—friends
and family, and you, O
Great Power and Source of
all life.
Help us to walk with you always.
For the soft wind and rain
that comes from the South,
we thank you, Our Creator.

Prayer Facing West
Creator of the setting sun,
We send our voice up to you.
We pray, Great Spirit, that
our journey through life
may know the harmony
and rhythm of the setting sun.
We pray that we may look
longingly toward the sunset
of our life, and feel
your greatness and beauty
within us.
For the sun's brilliance as
it sets in the west,
We thank you, Our Creator.

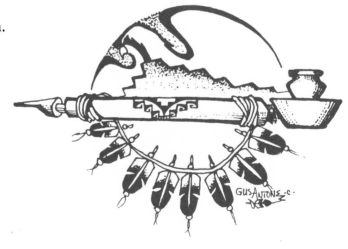

Prayer Facing North
Great God, Our Creator,
Our eyes are turned toward
you where you speak
to us from the North.
You are power over the

harshness of our lives,
stormy winds and great snows.
You are the Great One who
calms our fears and anxieties.
Give us strength and courage
to walk the strong winds
in life by walking with you.
For the protection you provide for us,
We thank you, Our Creator.

All join hands in a circle and recite **The Lord's Prayer.**

III.

Prayer to the Four Directions
(Face each direction in turn)

Petition to the East
Leader: Grandfather in the East: we offer you our thanksgiving and we honor you.
All: With your coming you waken all things; you bring all things from half-death with your light. You awaken the birds who praise you with song. You awaken the flowers who unfold their petals. You awaken the squirrel and the chipmunk to play. You awaken us refreshed and renewed to face another day; and you awaken the children with increased strength for greater good. You make light that which was dark. You restore us from that place of half-death to the world of the living.

As you make the world bright for us, let us enlighten our children so that they can see their way clearly. Permit us to pass to them the wisdom given us by our ancestors, so that the young, too, may grow strong and wise and kind and brave. May they awaken from good dreams to do good deeds.

Bless our babies and our children. They look to us for guidance, as we look to them with hope. That is our gift to them. May they cherish that gift and enlarge it.

Take our prayers to the Creator. We ask this through Christ our Lord. Amen.

Petition to the South
Leader: Grandmother in the South: we offer you our thanksgiving and we honor you.
All: If this summer past we have eaten well, traveled far, and seen our brothers and sister, if we have gathered medicines and harvested meat and fish and corn, it is because of your generosity. If we do not hunger and if we do not suffer hard times this coming winter, we owe our good fortune to you.

We come to you for guidance. As you have been kind to us, let us not be any less kind to our brothers and sisters, and strangers in spirit and deed. Let us bear the young and the old, the living and the dead, the well and the sick in our hearts. As you have nourished us, so let us feed the weak, the lame, and the sick; the widows and the orphans. Remind us to be strong. Walk this path with us.

Take pity on us; do not allow us to forget. Warm our hearts as you warm

mother earth, so that our thoughts may grow into good deeds just as the seed grows into corn. And should we falter, overlook our weakness.

Take our prayers to the Creator. We ask this through Christ our Lord. Amen.

Petition to the West

Leader: Grandfather in the West, we offer you our thanksgiving and we honor you.

All: Each day you remind us of life: with the sun's rise, birth and youth: with the sun's set, old age and death.

You remind us by the swiftness of the day how short life is. To see the sunrise and behold the sunset is a joy. To know life from its youth to its old age is a gift. You remind us of our destiny. When your skies glow, we know that your light will soon be gone. When the birds know that your light will dim, they sing sad songs. Flowers fold their petals, and the squirrels and chipmunks go to their nests. We, tired from our work, go to our rest. But we know that light will return.

Not so with life. No matter how much we may wish it to linger, we cannot hold back one day. And no matter how much we may wish to prolong our lives, we cannot hold back death. Like the day, so will men and women grow weak and die and proceed to the Land of Souls, where they will be united with their ancestors.

As your skies glow brightly just before sunset, may we, too, give light to our children. May our good deeds shine as brightly as the sun; and may we go to the Land of Souls with peace in our hearts.

May we sleep this night in the peace that you bring. May we have good dreams; and may we fulfill them when we wake.

Take our prayers to the Creator. We ask this through Christ our Lord. Amen.

Petition to the North

Leader: Grandmother in the North, we offer you thanksgiving and we honor you.

All: Temper your winds, your snows, and your storms so that we may survive, so that our children may not get sick, and so that our elderly may not suffer. We come to you for guidance. Help us to remember that if we are not wise, and if we fail to take care of tomorrow, we shall bear the consequences. Help us to make wise decisions.

Remember us and have compassion upon us when you come to test us, when you strip the trees of life, when you send us sickness and hardships; when you send the fish into the deep; when you drive the animals from their haunts. Be kind to our older brothers the moose, the deer, the bear, the beaver, and the squirrel. Keep them well and safe, for they too, must live.

Come not too quickly or too soon. Be not harsh. Stay not too long.

Bless our elders with the love of their grandchildren and the respect of all the people.

Take our prayers to the Creator. We ask this through Christ the Lord. Amen.

A Reading from the Sacred Scriptures (Zechariah 6:1-5 or one of your choice)

Concluding Prayer
Creator, giver of life, bring us

to new birth in water and
the Spirit.
Teach us the ways of peace
and forgiveness.
Help us to respect the differences
we see in one another and
learn to appreciate them.
As we become healers in
our relationships may we
come to wholeness and holiness.
Amen.

IV.

Scripture: Psalm 143:8-11

Oh, Great Spirit whose voice I hear in the winds,
Whose breath gives life to the world, hear me...
I come to you as one of your many children.
I am small and weak.
I need your strength and your wisdom.
May I walk in beauty.
Make my eyes ever behold the red and purple sunset.
Make my hands respect the things you have made,
And my ears sharp to your voice.
Make me wise so that I may know the thing you
have taught your children,
The lessons you have written in every leaf and rock.
Make me strong,
Not to be superior to my brothers and sisters, but to fight
my greatest enemy...
Myself...
Make me ever ready to come to you with straight eyes,
So that when life fades as the fading sunset,
My spirit may come to you without shame.

Song: *Peace Prayer*
(Copyright David Haas, 1957, words based on Navajo Prayer)

REFERENCES AND RESOURCES

Books

Alexander, Hartley Burr, *North American Mythology*, Cambridge, MA, University Press, 1932.

_____, *The World's Rim: Great Mysteries of the North American Indians*, Lincoln, NE, University of Nebraska Press, 1967.

Armstrong, V., *I Have Spoken: American History Through the Voices of the Indians*, Chicago, The Swallow Press, 1971.

Beck, Peggy V. and A. L. Walters, *The Sacred: Ways of Knowledge, Sources of Life*, Tsaile, AZ, Navajo Community College Press, 1977.

Berkhofer, Jr., Robert F., *The White Man's Indian: Images of the American Indian from Columbus to the Present*, New York, Random, 1979.

Bigfoot, D., *Parent Training for American Indian Families*, unpublished doctoral prospectus, Norman, OK, University of Oklahoma, 1987.

Boyd, Doug, *Rolling Thunder: A Personal Exploration into the Secret Healing Powers of an American Indian Medicine Man*, New York, Dell Books, 1974.

Brown, Dee, *Bury My Heart at Wounded Knee*, New York, Holt, Rinehart and Winston, 1971.

Brown, Joseph Epes, *The Spiritual Legacy of the American Indian*, Pamphlet No. 135, Wallingford, PA, Pendle Hill Publications, 1964.

_____, recorder and ed., *The Sacred Pipe: Black Elk's Account of the Seven Rites of the Oglala Sioux*, Norman, OK, University of Oklahoma Press, 1963. Reprint with new preface, New York, Penguin Books, 1971.

Brumble, H. David, III, *An Annotated Bibliography of American Indian and Eskimo Autobiographies*, Lincoln, NE, University of Nebraska Press, 1981.

Bryde, John F., *Modern Indian Psychology*, Vermillion, SD, Department of Indian Studies, University of South Dakota, 1971.

Buechel, Eugene, S.J., *A Dictionary of the Tetom Dakota Sioux Language*, edited by Paul Manhart, S.J., Pine Ridge, SD, Red Cloud Indian School, 1970.

Cash, Joseph H. and Herbert T. Hoover, *To Be an Indian: An Oral History*, New York, Holt, Rinehart and Winston, 1971.

Culin, Stewart, *Games of the North American Indians*, Washington, DC, Smithsonian Institution, Bureau of American Ethnology, Annual Report 24, 1907.

Curtis, Edward S., *The North American Indian*, vol. 3, 1908. Reprint, New York, Johnson Reprint Corporation, 1970.

Deloria, Vine, Jr., *Custer Died for Your Sins, an Indian Manifesto*, New York, Macmillan, 1969.

_____, *God Is Red*, New York, Grosset and Dunlap, 1973.

_____, *We Talk, You Listen*, New York, Macmillan, 1970.

_____, *The Nations Within: The Past and Future of American Indian Sovereignty*, New York, Pantheon, 1984.

Donavan, Vincent J., *The Church in the Midst of Creation*, Maryknoll, NY, Orbis Books, 1989.

Dorsey, George A., *The Arapaho Sun Dance: The Ceremony of the Offerings Lodge*, Publication 75, Anthropological Series 4, Chicago, Field Columbian Museum, 1903.

Drinnon, Richard, *Facing West: The Metaphysic of Indian Hating and Empire Building*, Westminster, MD, Schocken Books, 1990.

Eagle Man, Ed McGaa, *Mother Earth Spirituality: Native American Paths to Healing Ourselves and Our World*, San Francisco, Harper, 1990.

Eastman, Charles Alexander, *Indian Boyhood*, New York, McClure, Phillips, 1902.

_____, *The Soul of the Indian*, Boston, Houghton Mifflin, 1911.

_____, *From the Deep Woods to Civilization: Chapters in the Autobiography of an Indian*, Boston, Little, Brown, 1916.

Faith and Culture: A Multicultural Catechectical Resource Publication, No. 994-7, Washington, DC, U.S. Catholic Conference.

Fire, John (Lame Deer) and Richard Erdoes, *Lame Deer: Seeker of Visions*, New York, Simon and Schuster, 1972.

Fixico, D., *Termination and Relocations: Federal Indian Policy, 1945-1960*, Albuquerque, NM, University of New Mexico Press, 1986.

Forbes, Jack D., "Native Americans and Nixon: Presidential Politics and

Minority Self-Determination, 1969-1972," American Indian Studies Program, University of California, Los Angeles, out of print.

Foster, S. and M. Little, *The Book of the Vision Quest: Personal Transformation in the Wilderness*, New York, Prentice Hall, 1978.

Galeano, Eduardio, *Memory of Fire: Genesis*, NY, Pantheon, 1985.

Gill, Sam D., *Native American Religions: An Introduction*, Belmont, CA, Wadsworth, 1982.

Gittins, Anthony J., *Gifts and Strangers: Meeting the Challenge of Inculturation*, Mahwah, NJ, Paulist Press, 1989.

Goetzmann, William H., *Exploration and Empire: The Explorer and the Scientist in the Winning of the American West*, New York, Alfred A. Knopf, 1967.

Goodman, Jeffrey, *American Genesis: The American Indian and the Origins of Modern Man*, New York, Summit Books, 1981.

Graham, W.A., *The Custer Myth: A Source Book of Custeriana*, Harrisburg, PA, Stackpole, 1953.

Grim, John A., T*he Shaman: Patterns of Siberian and Ojibway Healing*, Norman, OK, University of Oklahoma Press, 1983.

Hammerschlag, C.A., *The Dancing Healers*, San Francisco, Harper & Row, 1988.

Hanson, W.D., *The Urban Indian*, San Francisco, San Francisco State University, 1980. ERIC Document Reproduction Service No. ED 231 587.

Hanke, Lewis, *Aristotle and the American Indians*, Bloomington, IN, Indiana University Press, 1974.

Hater, Robert J., *The Relationship between Evangelization and Catechesis*, clarification/study paper commissioned by the National Conference of Diocesan Directors of Religous Education, Washington, DC, 1981.

Highwalker, J., *Seeing with a Native Eye*, New York, Harper & Row, 1976, pp. 86-106.

Hill, Witt S., *Pressure Points in Growing Up Indian,* paper presented at 87th annual meeting of the American Psychological Association, New York City, August 1979.

Hudson, Charles, *The Southeastern Indians*, Knoxville, TN, University of Tennessee Press, 1976.

Hungry Wolf, A. and B. Hungry Wolf, *Children of the Sun*, New York, Morrow, 1987.

Jackson, Helen Hunt, *A Century of Dishonor*, (Reprint of 1881 edition), Williamstown, MA, Corner House Publishers, 1973.

Jacobs, W. R., *Dispossessing the American Indian.*, 2nd ed., Norman, OK, University of Oklahoma Press, 1985.

Jennings, Francis, *The Invasion of America: Indians, Colonialism and the Cant of Conquest*, Chapel Hill, University of North Carolina Press, 1975.

Johansen, Bruce E., *Forgotten Founders: How the American Indian Helped Shape Democracy*, Ipswich, MA, Gambit, 1982.

Johnston, Basil, *Ojibway Heritage*, New York, Columbia University Press, 1976.

Kaplan, B. and D. Johnson, "The Social Meaning of the Navaho Psychopathology and Psychotherapy," *Magic, Faith, and Healing*, A. Kiev, ed., New York, MacMillian, 1964, pp. 203-229.

Kraft, Charles H., *Christianity in Culture: A Study in Dynamic Biblical Theologizing in Cross-Cultural Perspective*, Maryknoll, NY, Orbis Books, 1979.

LaFromboise, T. D., *Circles of Women: Professionalization Training for American Indian Women*, Newton, MA, Women's Educational Equity Act, 1988.

_____, "Verbal Response Pattern of Effective American Indian Helpers," paper presented at annual meeting of the American Psychological Association, Los Angeles, August 1985.

Landes, Ruth, *Ojibwa Religion and the Midewiwin*, Madison, WI, University of Wisconsin Press, 1968.

Limerick, Patricia Nelson, *The Legacy of Conquest: The Unbroken Past of the American West*, New York, W.W. Norton, 1987.

Litkowski, M. Pelagia, *Kateri Tekakwitha, Joyful Lover*, Battle Creek, MI, Growth Unlimited, Inc., 1989.

Mails, Thomas E. and Dallas Chief Eagle, *Fools Crow*, Garden City, NY, Doubleday, 1979.

Manson, S. M. and J. E. Trimble, "American Indian and Alaska Native Communities: Past Efforts, Future Inquiries," *Reaching the Underserved: Mental Health Needs of Neglected Populations*, L.R. Snowden, ed., Newbury Park, CA, Sage, 1982.

Marriot, Alice and Carol K. Rachlin, *American Indian Mythology*, New York, Thomas Y. Crowell, 1968.

McLuhan, T.C., *Touch the Earth: A Self-Portrait of Indian Existence*, New York, Outerbridge and Lazard, 1971; Simon and Schuster, Pocket Books, 1972.

McGregor, James H., *The Wounded Knee Massacre From Viewpoint of the Sioux*, Baltimore, MD, Wirth Brothers, 1940.

Morey, S.M. and O. J. Gilliam, eds., *Respect for Life: The Traditional Upbringing of American Indian Children*, New York, Myrin Institute, 1974.

Murdock, George Peter and Timothy J. O'Leary, *Ethnographic Bibliography of North America*, 4th ed., 5 vols., New Haven, CT, Human Relations Area Files Press, 1975.

Neihardt, John G., *Black Elk Speaks: Being the Life Story of a Holy Man of the Ogalala Sioux*, New York, William Morrow, 1932. Reprints, Lincoln, NE, University of Nebraska Press. 1961, 1979.

O'Gorman, E., *The Invention of America*, Bloomington, IN, Indiana University Press, 1961.

Parker, Arthur C., "The Code of Handsome Lake, the Seneca Prophet," *New York State Museum Bulletin 163*, 1913. Reprinted in William N. Fenton, ed., *Parker on the Iroquois*, Syracuse, NY, Syracuse University Press, 1968.

Powell, Peter John, *Sweet Medicine: The Continuing Role of the Sacred Arrows, the Sun Dance, and the Sacred Buffalo Hat in Northern Cheyenne History*, 2nd vol., Norman, OK, University of Oklahoma Press, 1969.

Prucha, Francis Paul, ed., *The Indian in American History*, New York, Holt, Rinehart and Winston, 1971.

Radin, Paul, *The Story of the American Indian*, New York, Liveright Publishing Co., 1944.

_____, *The Road of Life and Death*, New York, Pantheon Books, 1945.

_____, *Crashing Thunder: The Autobiography of an American Indian*, New York and London, D. Appleton, 1926.

Rahner, Karl, "Concern for the Church," *Theological Investigations XX*, New York, Crossroad Publishing, 1981.

Red Horse, J., "American Indian Community Mental Health: A Primary Prevention Strategy," *New Directions in Prevention Among American Indian and Alaska Native Communities*, S. M. Manson, ed., Portland, OR, Oregon Health Sciences University, 1982.

Roest Crollius, Aru A., ed., *Effective Inculturation and Ethnic Identity, Inculturation*, working papers on Living, Faith and Culture, Rome, Pontifical Gregorian University, 1987.

Rosenfelt, Willard E., *The Last Buffalo; Cultural Views of the Sioux or Dakota Nation*, Minneapolis, MN, Denison, 1973. (Grades 4-7)

Ryan, R. A., "Strengths of the American Indian Family: State of the Art," *The American Indian Family: Strengths and Stresses*, F. Hoffman, ed., Isleta, NM, American Indian Social Research and Development Associates, 1980.

Shakespeare, Tom, *The Sky People*, New York, The Vantage Press, 1971. This book is written by an Arapaho Indian with a family tradition of Indian lore, and a good knowledge of anthropology.

Sharpe, J. Ed, ed., *American Indian Prayers and Poetry*, Cherokee, NC, Cherokee Publications, 1985.

Starkloff, Carl, "American Indian Religion and Christianity: Confrontation and Dialogue," Martin E. Marty and Dean Peerman, eds., *New Theology No. 9*, New York, Macmillan, 1972, pp. 121-150.

Steinmetz, Paul B., "Pipe, Bible and Peyote Among the Ogalala Lakota," *Stockholm Studies in Comparative Religion 19*, Motala, Sweden, 1980.

_____, *Meditations with Native Americas—Lakota Spirituality*, Santa Fe, NM, Bear and Co., 1984.

Storm, Hyemeyohsts, *Seven Arrows*, San Francisco, CA, Harper, 1972.

Sturevant, William C. and Bruce G. Trigger, eds., *Handbook of North American Indians*, vol. 15, Washington, DC, Smithsonian Institution, 1978.

Tooker, E., ed., *Native North American Spirituality of the Eastern Woodlands: Sacred Myths, Dreams, Visions, Speeches, Healing Formulas, Rituals and Ceremonials*, New York, Paulist Press, 1979.

Underhill, Ruth M., *Red Man's America*, Chicago, University of Chicago Press, 1971.

_____, *Red Man's Religion*, Chicago, University of Chicago Press, 1972. An excellent and sensitive account of basic concepts and traditions, with contemporary comments.

Unger, S., *The Destruction of American Indian Families*, New York, Association on American Indian Affairs, 1977.

U.S. Bureau of the Census, *A Statistical Profile of the American Indian Population: 1980 Census*, Washington, DC, U.S. Goverment Printing Offices, 1984.

Valle, R., *Cross-Cultural Competence in Minority Communities*, Chicago, University of Chicago Press, 1986.

Vecsey, Christopher, *Imagine Ourselves Richly: Mythic Narratives of North American Indians*, New York, Crossroads, 1988.

Vigenor, Gerald, (Chippewa/Ojibwa), novels and short stories.

Vogel, V.J., *The Rites of Passage*, Chicago, University of Chicago Press, 1987.

Walters, Anna Lee, *The Spirit of Native America: Beauty and Mysticism in American Indian Art*, San Francisco, Chronicle Books, 1989.

Weatherford, Jack, *Indian Givers: How the Indians of the Americas Transformed the World*, New York, Crown, 1988.

Weiser, Francis X., *Kateri Tekakwitha*, Caughnawaga, PQ, Canada, 1972.

Williams, Walter L., T*he Spirit and the Flesh: Sexual Diversity in American Indian Culture*, Boston, MA, Beacon Press, 1986.

Willoya, William and Vinson Brown, *Warriors of the Rainbow: Strange and Prophetic Indian Dreams*, Healdsburg, CA, Naturegraph, 1962.

Ywahoo, Khyani, *Voices of Our Ancestors*, Horticultural Hall, Boston, MA, Shambhala Publications, Inc., 1987.

Periodicals

"A Basic Call to Consciousness," *Akwesasne Notes*, New York, 1978.

"American Children: Overview of Developmental Issues," *Journal of Preventive Psychiatry*, vol. 1, 1982, pp. 319-330.

American Indian Culture and Research Journal, American Indian Studies Center, University of California, Los Angeles.

American Indian Quarterly: Journal of American Indian Studies, Native American Studies Program, University of California, Berkeley.

Beckwith, Martha Warren, "Mythology of the Oglala Dakota," *Journal of American Folk-Lore*, vol. 43, no. 170, October-December 1930, pp. 377-98.

Brod, R.L. and I. M. McQuiston, "American Indian Adult Education and Literacy: The First National Survey," *Journal of American Indian Education*, vol. 1, 1983, pp. 1-16.

Carlson, E., "Counselling in Native Context," *Canada's Mental Health*, vol. 23, pp. 7-9.

Coladarci, T., "High School Dropout Among Native Americans," *Journal of American Indian Education*, vol. 23, 1983, pp. 15-23.

Darou, W.G., "Counselling and the Northern Native," *Canadian Journal of Counseling*, vol. 21, 1978, pp. 33-41.

Dauphinais, P., T.D. LaFromboise and W. Rowe, "Perceived Problem and Sources of Help for American Indian Students," *Counselor Education and Supervision*, vol. 20, 1980, pp. 37-44.

Dorsey, James Owen, "Games of Dakota Children," *American Anthropologist*, vol. 4, 1891, pp. 329-45.

"Ethnic Minority Membership Increases in Conservation Denominations," *Christianity Today*, April 4, 1986.

Ford, R., "Counseling Strategies for the Ethnic Minority Student," Tacoma, WA, University of Puget Sound, 1983. ERIC Document Reproduction Service No. ED 247 504.

Gade, E., G. Hurlburt and D. Fuqua, "Study Habits and the Attitude of American Indian Students: Implications for Counselors," *School Counselor*, vol. 34, pp. 135-139.

Hoffman, T., R.H. Dana and B. Bottom, "Measured Acculturation and MMPI-168 Performance of the Native American Adults," *Journal of Cross-Cultural Psychology*, vol. 16, pp. 243-256.

Katz, P, "Psychotherapy with Native Americans Adolescents," *Canadian Journal of Psychiatry*, vol., 26, 1981, pp. 455-459.

La Fromboise, T. D., "Skills Training for Bicultural Competence: Rational and Application," *Journal of Counseling Psychology*, vol. 30, 1983, pp. 589-595.

"Native Americans Finding Place in Catholic Church," *National Catholic Register*, October 23, 1988.

Native Nation Right Fund Legal Review, contact NARF, 1506 Broadway, Boulder, CO 80302.

Native Nations Magazine, written and edited by American Indian people preparing for the Quincentenary. Writers include Leonard Peltier, John Mohawk, John Trudell, Suzan Shown Harjo and Robert Warrior. Contact Solidarity Foundation, 310 W. 52nd St., New York, NY 10019.

Plas, J.M. and W. Bellet, "Assessment of the Value-Attitude Orientations of American Indian Children," *Journal of School Psychology*, vol. 21, 1983, pp. 57-64.

Red Horse, J., R. G. Lewis, M. Fait and J. Decker, "Family Behavior of Urban American Indians," *Social Casework*, vol. 59, 1978, pp. 67-72.

Starkloff, Carl, "Keepers of the Tradition: The Symbol Power of Indigenous Ministry," *Kerygma*, Institute of Missions Studies, 223 Main, Ottawa, Ont. Canada K1S 1C4.

Organizations

Good Counsel Education Center
Good Counsel Drive
Mankato, MN 56001
(Videotape: *1492-1992 What's There to Celebrate* for high school)

Media Center
328 W. Kellogg Blvd.
St. Paul, MN 55102
(Series of filmstrips titled *A Look at Native Americans*)

Native American Authors Distribution Project
The Greenfield Review Press
2 Middle Grove Road, P.O. Box 308
Greenfield Center, NY 12833
(518) 584-1728/Fax (518) 583-9741
(Selection of poetry, fiction, nonfiction and storytelling)

Tekakwitha Conference National Center
P.O. Box 6768
Great Falls, MT 59406-6768
(Publications, video/slide presentation on Blessed Kateri)

Appendix

U.S. Bishops' Meeting/Native Americans

1992: Time for Remembering, Reconciling and Recommitting Ourselves as a People

The time has come "to look ahead to future challenges for our church and society in responding to the aspirations and needs of Native Americans," the U.S. bishops said in a statement released Dec. 17. The statement was on the agenda of the bishops' Nov. 11-14 meeting in Washington. But voting on the text took place on the meeting's final day when a number of bishops already had departed for home. With a two-thirds majority needed for approval, voting on the text was completed by mail. The final vote tally was 255-13. The statement, subtitled "Pastoral Reflections on the Fifth Centenary and Native American Peoples," says that "'all of us need to examine our own perceptions of Native Americans — how much they are shaped by stereotypes, distorted media portrayals or ignorance." The bishops called for Catholic "solidarity with the Native American community" and pledged to work on behalf of Native American needs in the areas of "health, housing, employment, education, poverty and other national issues." The bishops emphasized the importance of "inculturation of Catholic faith within the Native American community through a vital liturgical life, continuing educational efforts and creative pastoral ministry which demonstrate deep respect for native

culture and spiritualities, and which enhance fidelity to the Catholic faith." The bishops asked all believers to join in making the quincentennial year "a time of continuing conversion and reflection on the demands of the Gospel now as we seek to bring greater respect and justice to our ministry among Native Americans." The text of the statement follows.

Introduction

The fifth centenary of the coming of Europeans to this land is both a challenge and an opportunity, a time for looking back at where we have been and looking ahead to where we should be as a people and a nation. No specific aspect of this observance challenges us more than the situation of Native Americans in our midst — their past treatment, their current condition and their future aspirations.

As we prepare for the historic year of 1992, with both its opportunity for dialogue and its significant controversy, the Catholic community is blessed, enriched and profoundly challenged by the faith of Native Americans in our midst. We ask the Catholic community to join us in seek-

JANUARY 9, 1992
VOL. 21: NO. 31

origins

CNS documentary service

NATIVE AMERICANS — *from front page*
ing new understanding and awareness of their situation and in committing our church to new advocacy and action with our Native American brothers and sisters on issues of social justice and pastoral life which touch their lives.

In this effort, we build on our reflections of a year ago regarding the fifth centenary, "Heritage and Hope."[1] In these additional comments, we do not offer a comprehensive historical perspective but rather our reflections as pastors and teachers on the successes, failures and hopes that shape the relationship between our church and Native Americans.

We seek to speak not only to Native Americans, but to the whole church in this land. We speak as pastors, not only about important issues but first and foremost about a people — about our brothers and sisters whose dignity, culture and faith have too often been diminished and not adequately respected and protected by our civil society or our religious institutions. We seek to recognize and respond to the strengths of traditional Native American culture and spirituality, the pastoral and human needs of native peoples, the many pastoral efforts already under way and the continuing moral challenge of pursuing justice in the face of continuing discrimination.

In our letter on the fifth centenary, "Heritage and Hope," we sought to emphasize the ongoing challenge of evangelization, calling for continuing conversion to Jesus Christ and his values rather than emphasize a celebration of past events. We consider this historic year a time for sharing the Gospel with new energy and exploring its continuing demands. This fifth centenary should be a time for remembering, reconciling and recommitting ourselves as a church to the development of the people whose ancestors were here long before the first Europeans came to these shores 500 years ago.

I. A Time for Remembering

In this centennial year we recall the suffering of native peoples that followed the arrival of explorers and wave after wave of immigrants. We have spoken clearly about some of these failures in our letter on the fifth centenary. We repeat these strong words to remind ourselves of lessons which must be learned and commitments which must be kept as a part of this observance:

"As church, we often have been unconscious and insensitive to the mistreatment of our Native American brothers and sisters and have at times reflected the racism of the dominant culture of which we have been a part. In this quincentennial year, we extend our apology to our native peoples and pledge ourselves to work with them to ensure their rights, their religious freedom and the preservation of their cultural heritage" (Introduction).

In this letter, we point out that the coming of religious faith in this land began not 500 years ago, but centuries before in the prayers, chants, dance and other sacred celebrations of native people.

We also acknowledge that the encounter with the Europeans was often a "harsh and painful one" for native peoples, and we lament the diseases, death, destruction, injustices and disrespect for native ways and traditions which came with it. We recognize that:

"Often they (European Christians) failed to distinguish between what was crucial to the Gospel and what were matters of cultural preference. That failure brought with it catastrophic consequences for the native peoples, who were at times forced to become European at the same time they became Christian.

"Yet that is not the whole picture. The effort to portray the history of the encounter as a totally negative experience in which only violence and exploitation of the native peoples was present is not an accurate interpretation of the past" (p. 6; Origins, p. 416). Convinced of the saving truth of the Gospel and grateful for the sacrifices, care and concern of many missionaries for native people, we point out that "the expansion of Christianity into our hemisphere brought to the peoples of this land the gift of the Christian faith with its power of humanization and salvation, dignity and fraternity, justice and love" (p. 7; Origins p. 416).

"Our religious organizations, schools and other educational efforts must tell the truth about how Native Americans have been treated and how they have endured in this land."

We bishops urge that in 1992 our nation should give renewed attention to the condition of Native Americans:

"We encourage all Americans to better understand the role of native peoples in our history and to respond to the just grievances of our Native American brothers and sisters. We hope that this will be a graced time for rejecting all forms of racism" (p. 42; Origins, p. 424).

Now in these pastoral reflections we seek to offer some direction in realizing this hope. It is not enough for us simply to repeat strong words. The challenge of this historic year is not simply to look back, but also to look around at the current situation of native peoples and to look ahead to future challenges for our church and society in responding to the aspirations and needs of Native Americans.

II. A Time for Reconciliation

We have also called for "new reconciliation in the spirit of the Gospel among all Americans and to recognize more fully our solidarity" (p. 43; Origins, p. 424). The challenge of reconciliation in Jesus Christ requires greater awareness and understanding, increased dialogue and interaction, and a commitment to mutual respect and justice among diverse peoples. Most Americans know almost nothing about the lives

The U.S. bishops' November 1990 pastoral letter for the 1992 observances of the fifth centenary of evangelization in the Americas appeared in Origins, Vol. 20, pp. 413ff.

"The encounter with the Europeans was a harsh and painful one for the indigenous peoples," the pastoral letter said. It described the introduction of diseases, cultural oppression, injustice, disrespect for native ways and traditions. "The great waves of European colonization were accompanied by destruction of Indian civilization, the violent usurpation of Indian lands and the brutalization of their inhabitants," the pastoral said. "Many of those associated with the colonization of the land failed to see in the natives the workings of the same God that they espoused."

Still, the text said, "there was, in fact, a deeply positive aspect of the encounter of European and American cultures." The "Gospel did in fact take root.... It cannot be denied that the interdependence of the cross and the crown that occurred during the first missionary campaigns brought with it contradictions and injustices. But neither can it be denied that the expansion of Christianity into our hemisphere brought to the peoples of this land the gift of the Christian faith with its power of humanization and salvation, dignity and fraternity, justice and love."

495

For a recent text of current interest, see "An Apology to Native Peoples," by Canada's Missionary Oblates of Mary Immaculate, in Origins, the current volume, pp. 183f.

The July 1991 statement by the Oblates said that "after 150 years of being with and ministering to the native peoples of Canada" the order wished "to offer an apology for certain aspects of that presence and ministry."

"Recent criticisms of Indian residential schools and the exposure of instances of physical and sexual abuse within these schools" were among circumstances that led to the apology, the statement said. It said too that "anthropological and sociological insights of the late 20th century have shown how deep, unchallenged and damaging was the naive cultural, ethnic, linguistic and religious superiority complex of Christian Europe when its peoples met and interrelated with the aboriginal peoples of North America."

"A certain healing" is needed before "a new and more truly cooperative phase of history can occur," the statement said. It added:

"We apologize for the part we played in the cultural, ethnic, linguistic and religious imperialism that was part of the mentality with which the peoples of Europe first met the aboriginal peoples and which consistently has lurked behind the way the native peoples of Canada have been treated by civil governments and by the churches. We were, naively, part of this mentality and were, in fact, often a key player in its implementation. We recognize that this mentality has from the beginning and ever since continually threatened the cultural, linguistic and religious traditions of the native peoples.

"We recognize that many of the problems that beset native communities today — high unemployment, alcoholism, family ▶

and history of the first Americans. Our religious organizations, schools and other educational efforts must tell the truth about how Native Americans have been treated and how they have endured in this land. History can be healing if we will face up to its lessons.

All of us need to examine our own perceptions of Native Americans — how much they are shaped by stereotypes, distorted media portrayals or ignorance. We fear that prejudice and insensitivity toward native peoples is deeply rooted in our culture and in our local churches. Our conference has consistently condemned racism of every kind, and we renew our call for increased efforts to overcome prejudice and discrimination as they touch our Native American brothers and sisters.

This reconciliation should also reflect the realities of Native American life today, in our nation and our church. The Native American community now includes almost 2 million Indians, Eskimos and Aleuts, including a number of Hispanic people who also identify themselves as Indians. Native Americans are both citizens of the United States and members of their tribes, pueblos or nations. Native Americans are among the fastest growing populations in our country. They constitute a vital, diverse and growing community.

Native Americans are present in every state. The largest number are found in Oklahoma where many tribes were relocated. While a majority of Native Americans live in the Western part of the United States, North Carolina has the fifth largest Indian population in the country. Only Oklahoma, California, Arizona and New Mexico have larger populations. Moreover, well over a third of all Native Americans now reside in large cities. Native American people are an integral part of many of our metropolitan areas, especially in the Midwest and West.

One in four Native Americans is poor. Many struggle with the realities of inadequate housing, joblessness, health problems including the disease of alcoholism. While significant numbers of Native Americans have become lawyers, doctors, artists and other professionals, many others live with dashed hopes and bleak futures as a result of discrimination, lack of opportunity and economic powerlessness.

Within our family of faith we are very blessed to have significant numbers of Native American Catholics, now numbering more than a quarter of a million. Our church is blessed with two Native American bishops, more than two dozen priests, many deacons, 90 sisters and brothers and many lay leaders.

There are a variety of significant initiatives focused on the pastoral life and needs of Native American Catholics:

—For more than a century, the Bureau of Catholic Indian Missions has through the generosity of U.S. Catholics served the pastoral and spiritual needs of Native American Catholics providing for Native American ministries providing more than $3 million annually.

—The Tekakwitha Conference provides

an important voice and gathering place for those who serve the Native American Catholic community.

—Many dioceses have undertaken creative efforts, and religious communities have established ministries to serve the needs of Native American Catholics.

—Our own national conference of bishops has previously developed and adopted a major statement on the church and American Indians outlining pastoral priorities and a social-justice agenda that still are valid today.[2]

—Several dioceses and state Catholic conferences have also made justice for Native Americans a major ecclesial priority.

In this task of reconciliation, the persistence and vitality of Catholic faith in the Native American community is an irreplaceable asset. We are one family united in faith, citizenship and humanity. However, the Native American Catholic community faces three special and related challenges:

"In liturgical, pastoral and spiritual life, we seek a genuine reconciliation between the essential traditions of Catholic faith and the best of the traditions of Native American life, each respecting, shaping and enriching the other."

A. Inculturation

The church is called to bring the saving word of the Gospel to every people and culture. Our goal must be an authentic inculturation of Catholic faith within the Native American community through a vital liturgical life, continuing educational efforts and creative pastoral ministry which demonstrate deep respect for native culture and spiritualities and which enhance fidelity to the Catholic faith.

This is not an easy or simple task. Authentic inculturation moves in three integral steps: 1) The culture which the Word of God encounters is challenged and purified by that Word; 2) the best of the culture is enhanced by the truth of the Gospel; 3) the church is enriched by respecting the culture which the Gospel embraces and which in turn embraces the Gospel.

This task of inculturation is not an unprecedented or new challenge, but it remains an essential step toward an authentic Catholic Native American community within the structure and bonds of the universal church. As Pope John Paul II has said:

"When the church enters into contact with cultures, the church must welcome all that is compatible with the Gospel in these traditions of the peoples in order to bring the richness of Christ to them and to be enriched herself by the manifold wisdom of the nations of the earth" (Pope John Paul II, discourse to the Pontifical Council for Cultures, Jan. 17, 1987).

In liturgical, pastoral and spiritual life, we seek a genuine reconciliation between the essential traditions of Catholic faith and the best of the traditions of Native American life, each respecting, shaping and enriching the other. Native American Catholics are called to be both true Catholic believers and authentic Native Americans. Far from being incompatible, these two traditions — the Catholic way and the native way — enrich each other and the whole church.

Our challenge is to make sure that a truly Catholic religious culture interfaces with truly Native American cultures. A highly secularized society can overshadow a Catholic and Native American sense of mystery when encountering God, the created world and human life.

We call on liturgists, theologians and pastoral leaders to help us address these real issues as we shape a Native American expression of faith that is authentically Catholic and deeply Native American. It is our responsibility as bishops to encourage and supervise the presentation of the faith in liturgy and catechetics which safeguard Catholic tradition and native ways.

"We also renew our commitment to press for justice in the prompt and fair adjudication of treaty rights."

B. Participation

This challenge will require an ongoing effort to increase the participation of Native Americans in the life of the church. We need to hear clearly the voice of Catholic Native Americans. We need their leadership in the dialogue that can take place between Native American traditionalists and the church. We welcome their gifts and contributions. We need their active participation in the ministries and life of the church. We ask their advice about the ways the whole Catholic community can best respond to the realities of injustice and ignorance and their impact on native peoples. We advocate full opportunities for native people and we seek new partnerships with them in building the body of Christ within the Native American community.

C. Pastoral Leadership

We especially need to call forth and support the leadership of Native Americans — as priests, religious and lay leaders. We are already blessed with many faithful and creative leaders, but more are needed to preach the Gospel and serve the needs of the Native American communities. We continue to welcome the generosity and commitment of many non-Native Americans who serve this community, but we look forward to the time when Native American bishops, priests, deacons, sisters, brothers and lay leaders will increasingly shape and carry out the work of the church in the Native American community and in the larger Catholic communi-

ty. All those who serve within the Native American Catholic community should be well trained in Catholic theology and Native American culture and ways.

We pray that the blessings of the past and the hard work of the present will yield an even more vibrant and faithful Catholic Native American community. We strongly support the impressive efforts under way to train and prepare Native Americans for leadership in the priesthood, diaconate, religious life and lay ministries.

In all these efforts we will build on our past and current pastoral ministries, educational commitments and spiritual care within the Native American community. We acknowledge the failure and misguided direction of some past efforts, but we also recognize the enormous contributions of Indian schools, parishes and ministries in meeting the needs of the Native American community and developing leaders from among their number. More authentic inculturation, increased participation and stronger pastoral leadership will strengthen the faith of not only our Native American sisters and brothers, but our entire family of faith in the United States.

III. A Time for Recommitment
A. Public Advocacy

As we seek to respond to these ecclesial challenges, we also recommit ourselves to stand with native peoples in their search for greater justice in our society. We seek to be advocates with native leaders in this effort, not simply advocates for their needs. Together we must call our nation to greater responsiveness to the needs and rights of native people. We recognize that there are groups working for justice and cultural recognition for native peoples at regional and global levels. We encourage these efforts to build bridges among the indigenous people in the Americas and throughout the world.

We once again commit ourselves as the National Conference of Catholic Bishops to recognize and act upon the Native American dimensions of our ongoing advocacy regarding health, housing, employment, education, poverty and other national issues. No group is touched more directly by federal policy than Native Americans. We must be alert and active regarding federal policies which support or undermine Native American lives, dignity and rights. As a church committed to a "preferential option for the poor and vulnerable," we recognize that Native Americans are often the most poor and vulnerable in our midst. We shall actively support initiatives to meet housing, health and employment needs of native people, with a priority for measures that increase self-sufficiency and economic empowerment.

B. Respecting Treaty Rights

We also renew our commitment to press for justice in the prompt and fair adjudication of treaty rights. These treaties for which Native American tribes gave up their homelands, keeping only a fraction of what they originally inhabited, are of prime concern to their descendants. In some important ways they are now receiving some greater recognition of their rights, but agencies of government and courts do not always recognize the complexities of tribal autonomy within the territories of sovereign states. Native Americans have the right to be self-determining, to decide the ways their land and natural resources on those lands are used for the benefit of their people and for the broader common good.

C. Ongoing Support for Native American Communities

Our Campaign for Human Development has supported the quest for justice and self-help among native peoples. In its brief history, CHD has provided almost $3.5 million to support more than 100 projects focused on stewardship of Indian land and resources, restoration of tribal recognition and rights, cultural preservation and increased accountability for tribal education, welfare and legal systems. We support continued efforts to empower and assist Native Americans in their search for justice. We also renew our support for the Bureau of Catholic Indian Missions and its essential work of evangelization and pastoral care within the Native American community. The American Board of Catholic Missions and the Catholic Church Extension Society also supply valuable assistance and help to the Native American Catholic community. Their support for the church's work is a crucial resource building a vibrant Catholic faith within our dioceses and parishes which serve native people.

IV. A Call to Action

The Catholic community and our bishops' conference are called in this historic year to join together in renewed efforts to address several important areas which affect our Native American brothers and sisters. We call on the relevant committees of our conference of Catholic bishops to integrate the needs and contributions of native Catholics into their ongoing agenda. Significant work has been done in approving translations of eucharistic prayers, in public policy, in pastoral and social-justice efforts, but more is required. Questions of Native American inculturation need to be further addressed by our liturgy and pastoral practices committees; advocacy and empowerment by our domestic policy and the Campaign for Human Development committees; pastoral leadership by our Committees on Vocations, Priestly Life and Ministry, Priestly Formation and Permanent Diaconate; Indian education by our education committee. We also propose for consideration the establishment of an ad hoc NCCB Committee on Native American Catholics to help oversee this effort and to coordinate our conference's response to this statement.

Finally, we ask all believers to join with us in making this centennial year a time of continuing conversion and reflection on the demands

of the Gospel now as we seek to bring greater respect and justice to our ministry among Native Americans. As we said a year ago: "Evangelization is unfinished if exploitation of the weak, of minorities still exists. The quincentenary calls us to a new commitment as Christians to right the evils of the past and the present, and to be forceful advocates of the peace and justice proclaimed by the Gospel.... Our observances should include times of mourning over the injustices of the past and vital efforts at reconciliation with our Native American brothers and sisters through prayer and social action" (p. 45; Origins, pp. 424 and 425). This historic year calls us to both reflection and action concerning the most effective ways we can seek justice and build up the body of Christ within the Native American community.

"We recognize that Hispanic and African Americans share with native peoples the reality of discrimination and the challenge of achieving full acceptance in our society and church.... Ties of solidarity and common struggle can help these communities work together to assist the church in recognizing diversity as a strength and gift."

We recognize that Hispanic and African Americans share with native peoples the reality of discrimination and the challenge of achieving full acceptance in our society and church. A significant number of Hispanic people share roots and cultural ties with native peoples, as do some African Americans. These ties of solidarity and common struggle can help these communities work together to assist the church in recognizing diversity as a strength and gift. Native, Hispanic and African American members of our communities are called to be leaders and allies in the task of shaping a truly "Catholic" community — open to all God's children.

Conclusion

When he came to our land four years ago, Pope John Paul II affirmed and challenged Native American Catholics as he still challenges all of us in this fifth centenary year:

"I encourage you as native people to preserve and keep alive your cultures, your languages, the values and customs which have served you well in the past and which provide a solid foundation for the future. Your encounter with the Gospel has not only enriched you; it has enriched the church. We are well aware that this has not taken place without its difficulties and, occasionally, its blunders. However ... the Gospel does not destroy what is best in you. On the contrary, it enriches the spiritual qualities and gifts that are distinctive of your cultures....

"Here I wish to urge the local churches to be truly 'catholic' in their outreach to native peoples and to show respect and honor for their culture and all their worthy traditions.... All consciences must be challenged. There are real injustices to be addressed and biased attitudes to be challenged."

Solidarity with the Native American community is a special challenge for our church in this fifth centenary year. We ask the intercession of Blessed Kateri Tekakwitha and Blessed Juan Diego as we seek to recognize the burdens of history and meet the challenges of today. We hope and pray that 1992 will be a time for remembering, for genuine reconciliation and recommitment to work for greater justice for the descendants of the first Americans.

Footnotes

[1] Heritage and Hope: Evangelization in the United States, pastoral letter on the fifth centenary of evangelization in the Americas, National Conference of Catholic Bishops, 1990.

[2] Statement of the U.S. Catholic Bishops on American Indians, 1977. ▨